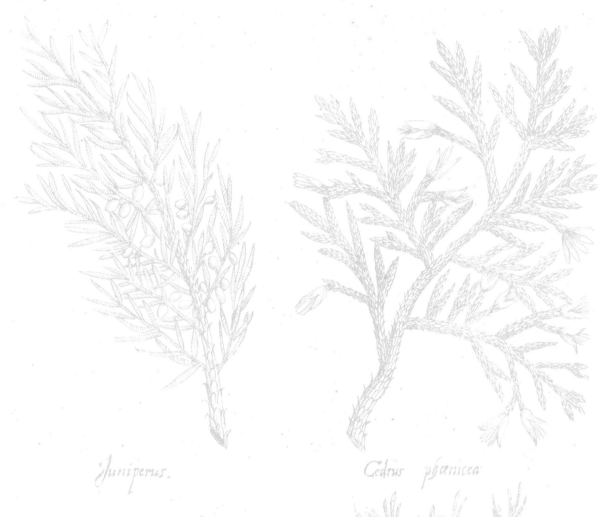

Juniperus.   Cedrus phænicea

A Cross-Stitch
CHRISTMAS®

EDITOR-IN-CHIEF
BEVERLY RIVERS

MANAGING EDITOR   ART DIRECTOR
JULIE BURCH KEITH   PATRICIA CHURCH PODLASEK

A CROSS-STITCH CHRISTMAS® EDITOR   EVE MAHR
ASSISTANT ART DIRECTOR   CHERIE DeTOLVE-DALE

CROSS-STITCH & NEEDLEWORK® EDITOR   NANCY R. WYATT
ASSOCIATE EDITOR   BARBARA HICKEY
ASSISTANT ART DIRECTOR   PATTY CRAWFORD
EDITORIAL ASSISTANT   MARY JOHNSON
ILLUSTRATOR   CHRIS NEUBAUER GRAPHICS
PHOTOGRAPHER   PERRY STRUSE

PUBLISHING DIRECTOR   WILLIAM R. REED
PUBLISHER   MAUREEN RUTH
MARKETING MANAGER   DALE ENGELKEN
BUSINESS MANAGER   CATHY BELLIS
PRODUCTION DIRECTOR   DOUGLAS M. JOHNSTON
PRODUCTION MANAGER   PAM KVITNE
ASSISTANT PREPRESS MANAGER   MARJORIE J. SCHENKELBERG
MARKETING ASSISTANT   KRISTI HASEK

VICE PRESIDENT
JERRY WARD

Meredith
CORPORATION

CHAIRMAN AND CEO
WILLIAM T. KERR

CHAIRMAN OF THE EXECUTIVE COMMITTEE
E.T. MEREDITH III

MEREDITH PUBLISHING GROUP

PUBLISHING GROUP PRESIDENT   CHRISTOPHER M. LITTLE
CREATIVE SERVICES   ELLEN DE LATHOUDER
MANUFACTURING   BRUCE HESTON
CONSUMER MARKETING   KARLA JEFFRIES
GROUP SALES   JERRY KAPLAN
INTEGRATED MARKETING   BOB MATE
STRATEGIC MARKETING   BILL MURPHY
INTERACTIVE MEDIA   HAL ORINGER
OPERATIONS   DEAN PIETERS
FINANCE   MAX RUNCIMAN
LICENSING AND NEW MEDIA   THOMAS L. SLAUGHTER

Member
HIA
HOBBY INDUSTRY
ASSOCIATION

Our Mark of Excellence seal assures you that every project in this book has been constructed and checked under the direction of the crafts experts at *Better Homes and Gardens® Cross Stitch & Needlework®* magazine.

For book editorial questions, write
Better Homes and Gardens A Cross Stitch Christmas, 1716 Locust St.–GA 308, Des Moines, IA 50309-3023;
phone 515/284-3623; fax 515/284-3884.
For additional copies or billing questions,
call 800/322-0691.

ISSN: 1081-468X
ISBN: 0-696-21209-9

For cross-stitchers,
Christmas is timeless.

To make the day special, we prepare for

Christmas year round, choosing perfect patterns,

shopping for the right materials, and allotting precious time for

stitching. We stitch with our hands—and our hearts—to create

treasures that will be cherished, not just for a season, but for

many Christmases to come. With that in mind, we chose

this collection of designs reflecting a variety of styles—from

whimsical to traditional, from simple to elaborate—all of them

classic in appeal. We hope that you will enjoy stitching these

spirited decorations and festive gifts every day of the year and

that all of your holiday projects become

Timeless Treasures.

Contents

Page 39

Page 40

Page 117

Page 14

4

Page 64

Page 98

Page 11

Page 85

As we celebrate

the first Christmas

of a new millennium, let the

holiday themes and

needlework techniques of

bygone days inspire

your stitches.

~

Christmas
Past and
Present

Hardanger nearly became extinct in the
mid-1900s. A form of needle lace, it evolved over many
centuries in Norway and spread to other parts of Scandinavia. Brought to the New World by 19th-century
settlers, it adorned everything from dish towels to wedding dresses. In the United States, it remained virtually
unknown outside ethnic communities until it was revived by cross-stitch designers searching
for other counted thread techniques. Celebrate the first Christmas of the 21st century by stitching a lacy
Hardanger bellpull, accented with poinsettias and a message of peace, on 28-count Jobelan.

By the dawn of the 20th century, the development of color printing presses made
greeting cards abundant and inexpensive. Before telephones and automobiles were common,
penny postcards were a popular form of holiday greeting for distant family and friends.
Nearly 100 years after a 9-year-old girl named Helen received this Santa card from her cousins in 1911,
its charm is captured in cross-stitch by the granddaughter of the recipient.

Designs: Postcard Santa, Laurie Duvall; Poinsettia Bellpull, Friends in Needlework, adapted by Laurie Duvall

*B*lackwork had it's heyday in Elizabethan England,
*a time when only high nobility was allowed to wear real lace. Clever seamstresses used
black thread and simple stitches to create lacy patterns on white fabric, creating what was known as
"poor man's lace." Today the same patterns worked in vivid colors add a rich accent to the Christmas tree.*

*I*n the December 1934 issue of Better Homes and Gardens® magazine,
*Garden Clubs Editor, Cousin Marion, told Christmas legends about Harz Mountain fir trees. In one story the fir
trees protected canaries from a fierce storm. In another a tree showered an impoverished peasant with
so many pinecones she could hardly carry them. When she arrived home, she discovered they had turned to pure
silver, thus saving her family at Christmas. These stories inspired this contemporary wreath of golden canaries
and glittering pinecones stitched on 25-count Lugana. As a variation, stitch any of the birds alone for an ornament.*

Designs: Blackwork Ornaments, Joan Beiriger; Canaries and Pinecones, Barbara Sestok

Poet Clement Moore and cartoonist Thomas Nast created

the American Santa Claus—plump, rosy-cheeked, and dressed in a red suit. Europeans, however,

pictured St. Nicholas as an old man in a long coat, often carrying a tall cane or crosier, the image

of his 4th-century namesake, Bishop Nicholas of Myra. In those traditions, Christmas celebrations

began on December 25, so St. Nick brought the trees, wreaths, and other greens for holiday

decorating—as well as gifts—on Christmas Eve. Stitch one or both of these old-world Santas,

laden with historic charm, on 32-count linen, to warm your holiday home.

Designs: Laura Doyle; Blue Santa, adapted by Lynn Daugherty; Green Santa, adapted by Laurie Duvall

Christmas Past and Present

Monograms, *personalized marks created by*
combining initials, have been around for centuries. Victorian needleworkers
were especially fond of linens monogrammed or initialed with curvy scripts.
They would have appreciated these companion alphabets. Each letter
is pretty enough to stitch singly, and they're scaled to combine in traditional
form with first and middle (or maiden) initial on either side of the surname
initial. A few suggestions are pictured here: A purse to wear as jewelry or hang on a tree, a
dainty sachet to share as a gift, or a tiny brooch for yourself, the flower-trimmed banding cuff for an embossed
velvet stocking, and a personalized cover for a prayer book, Bible, journal, or other special tome.

Designs: Victorian Monograms, Donna Yuen

Hardanger Bellpull

Supplies
*12×18" piece of 28-count white
    Jobelan fabric*
Cotton embroidery floss
Weeks Dyeworks overdyed floss
White #8 and #12 pearl cotton
Mill Hill seed beads
Purchased 6"-wide bellpull hardware

Stitches
Measure 4" from the edges on the top corner of the fabric; begin working buttonhole edge there, referring to the diagram. Work the cross-stitches using three plies of floss. Work the satin-stitch Kloster blocks over the number of threads indicated on the chart. For the Algerian eyelets, give each stitch a gentle tug to open a small hole.

Cut away the threads for the woven areas of the design, referring to the diagram. Work woven bars with picots over the exposed threads. Attach the seed beads using two plies of floss. Press the finished stitchery facedown on a soft towel.

Assembly
At the top of the bellpull, trim away excess fabric 1" beyond the stitching. For the sides and bottom, trim the fabric close to the stitching.

Press the top edge of the fabric under ¼". Slip the fabric through the bellpull hardware and hand-stitch the folded edge to the back of the fabric.

Postcard Santa

Supplies
*22×27" piece of 28-count olive green
    Cashel linen*
Cotton embroidery floss
*1 additional skein each of white and
    black-brown (DMC 3371) floss*
Kreinik blending filament
Desired frame

Stitches
Center and stitch the design, *pages 18–20,* on the linen. Use three plies of floss to work the stitches over two threads of the fabric unless otherwise specified. Press the stitchery from the back. Frame the piece as desired.

Blackwork Ornaments

Supplies
For each ornament
*10×12" piece of 25-count white
    Jobelan fabric*
Cotton embroidery floss
Mill Hill seed beads
Tracing paper
Erasable fabric marker
*5×6" piece each of self-stick mounting
    board with foam and felt*
*⅝ yard of ¼"-diameter burgundy
    twisted cord*
Crafts glue

Stitches
Center and stitch the design from the desired chart, *page 21,* onto the fabric. Use two plies of floss to work the stitches over the number of threads indicated on the chart. Attach the seed beads using two plies of floss. Press the stitchery facedown on a soft towel.

Assembly
Use the erasable marker to draw an outline around the stitched area of the design as indicated by the dashed line on the chart; *do not* cut out. Place the tracing paper over the fabric and trace the ornament outline. Cut out the paper pattern. Use the paper pattern to cut matching shapes from the mounting board and the felt.

Peel the protective paper from the mounting board. Center the foam side on the back of the stitchery and press to stick. Trim the excess fabric

Continued on page 21

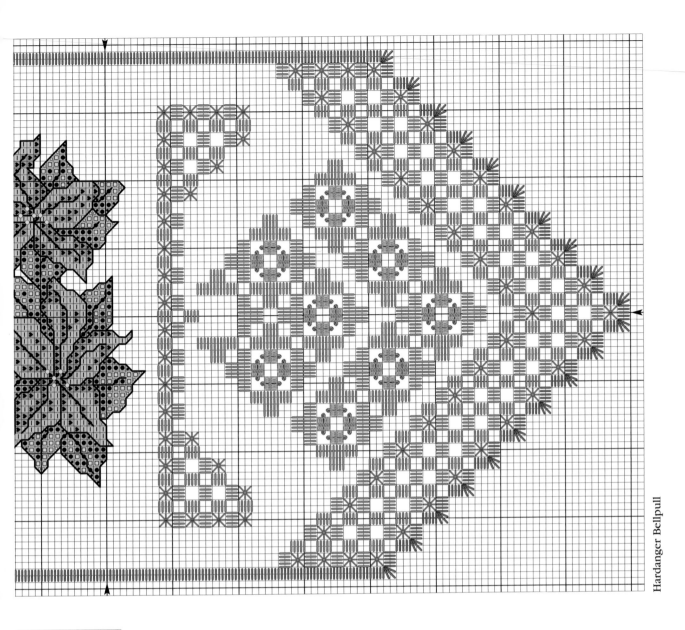

Hardanger Bellpull

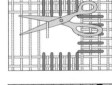

Removing Threads

Kloster Blocks

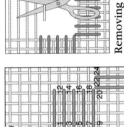

Algerian Eyelet

Buttonhole Stitch

Step 1

Step 2

Step 3

Woven Bars with Picots

Weeks Dyeworks
Overdyed Floss

Anchor		DMC	
	✕	2264	Garnet
1005	▯	498	Christmas red
045	▶	814	Garnet
1044	●	895	Dark hunter green
268	▫	3345	Medium hunter green

BACKSTITCH (1X)

382 ╱ 3371 Black-brown – all stitches

BUTTONHOLE STITCH (1X)

002 000 White #8 pearl cotton

ALGERIAN EYELET (1X)

002 ✳ 000 White #12 pearl cotton

SATIN STITCH (1X)

002 000 White #8 pearl cotton

WOVEN BARS WITH PICOT (1X)

002 000 White #12 pearl cotton

MILL HILL BEADS

⦿ 00557 Gold seed beads

Stitch count: 160 high x 78 wide

Finished design sizes:
28-count fabric – 11½ x 5½ inches
32-count fabric – 10 x 4⅞ inches
36-count fabric – 8⅞ x 4⅓ inches

Christmas Past and Present

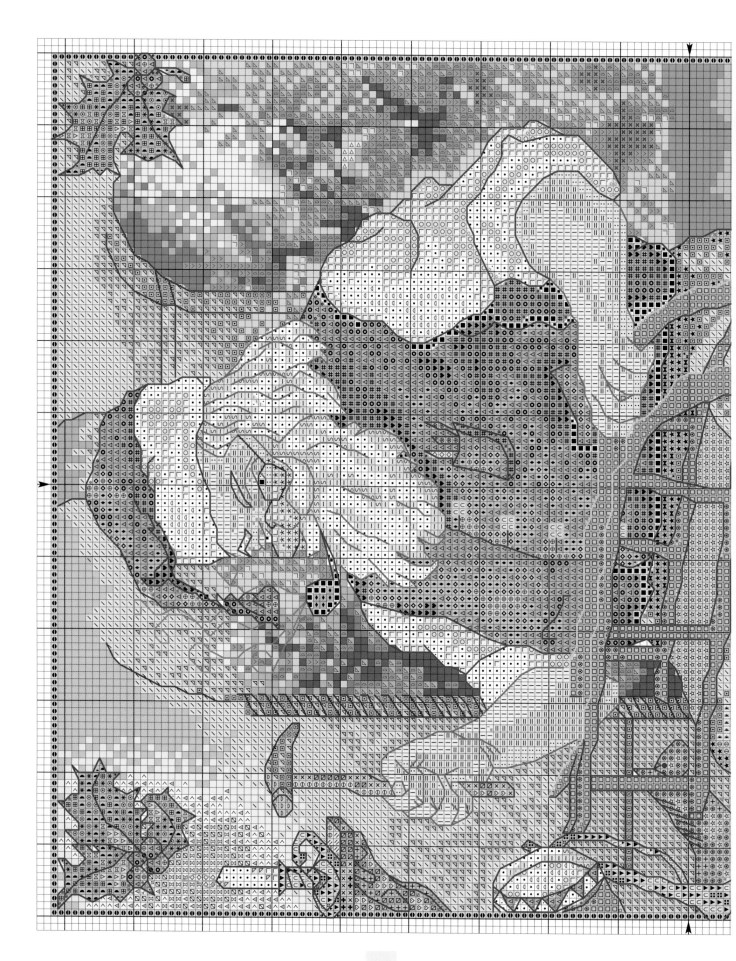

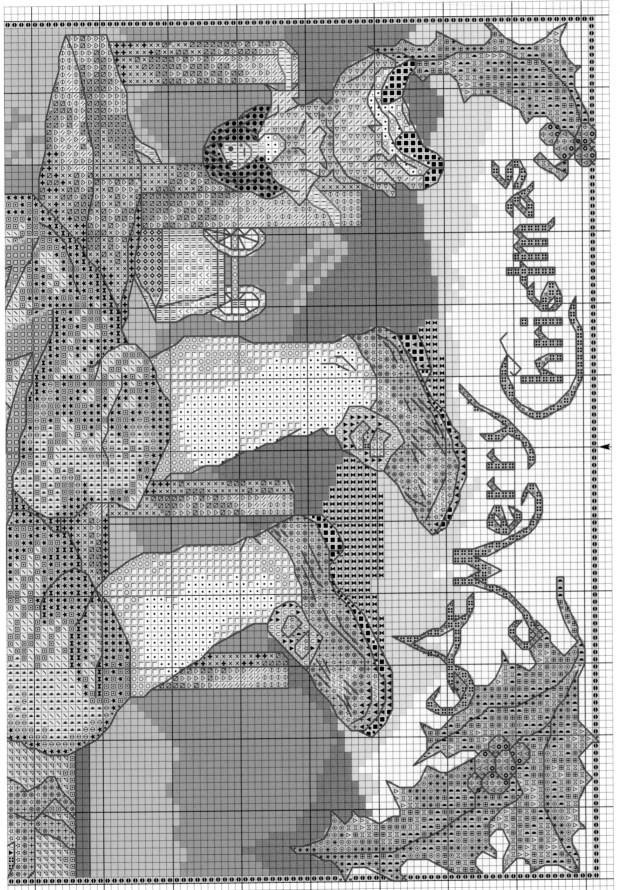

Postcard Santa

Christmas Past and Present

Postcard Santa

Anchor		DMC
002	·	000 White
290	II	307 True lemon
9046	△	321 True Christmas red
1025	◆	347 Deep salmon
235	⊠	414 Dark steel
398	○	415 Light pearl gray
374	×	420 Medium hazel
372	♡	422 Light hazel
371	▲	433 Dark chestnut
370	☐	434 Medium chestnut
1046	+	435 Light chestnut
1045	⊛	436 Dark tan
362	☆	437 Medium tan
288	∧	445 Light lemon
1005	◉	498 Dark Christmas red
8581	▣	646 Medium beaver gray
1040	◪	647 True beaver gray
900	◿	648 Light beaver gray
923	✳	699 Dark Christmas green
227	◉	701 True Christmas green
887	∼	739 Pale tan
302	◇	743 True yellow
868	≡	754 Peach
9575	⠒	758 Light terra-cotta
1022	✶	760 True salmon
234	⅂	762 Pale pearl gray
358	●	801 Coffee brown
043	#	815 Medium garnet
390	−	822 Pale beige-gray
1041	★	844 Deep beaver gray
375	✚	869 Dark hazel
897	♥	902 Deep garnet
258	◗	904 Deep parrot green
257	⊞	905 Dark parrot green
256	⋈	906 Medium parrot green
255	▽	907 Light parrot green
1010	⊡	951 Ivory
075	◈	962 Medium rose-pink
073	◻	963 Pale rose-pink

391	S	3033 Pale mocha
886	◣	3046 Yellow-beige
1024	◈	3328 Dark salmon
862	∩	3348 Light yellow-green
382	■	3371 Black-brown
1023	⊕	3712 Medium salmon
1020	L	3713 Pale salmon
025	◁	3716 Light rose-pink
373	◺	3828 True hazel
901	●	3829 Deep old gold

BLENDED NEEDLE

002 234	◥	000 White (2X) and 762 Pale pearl gray (1X)
002 386	◿	000 White (2X) and 3823 Pale yellow (1X)
370 397	◐	434 Medium chestnut (1X) and 3072 Pale beaver gray (2X)
370 382	◆	434 Medium chestnut (2X) and 3371 Black-brown (1X)
1045 397	k	436 Dark tan (1X) and 3072 Pale beaver gray (2X)
1040 397	▽	647 True beaver gray (1X) and 3072 Pale beaver gray (2X)
1041 382	⋈	844 Deep beaver gray (2X) and 3371 Black-brown (1X)
290	⊠	307 True lemon (2X) and 091 Kreinik Star yellow blending filament (1X)
288	☑	445 Light lemon (2X) and 091 Kreinik Star yellow blending filament (1X)
300	△	745 Light yellow (2X) and 091 Kreinik Star yellow blending filament (1X)
886 386	⊖	3046 Yellow-beige (1X) and 3823 Pale yellow (2X)
386	▷	3823 Pale yellow (2X) and 091 Kreinik Star yellow blending filament (1X)
306	▼	3820 Dark straw (2X) and 202HL Kreinik Aztec gold #4 very-fine braid (1X)
901	⊞	3829 Deep old gold (2X) and 202HL Kreinik Aztec gold #4 very-fine braid (1X)

HALF CROSS-STITCH (2X)
Stitch in this direction ╱

215	▨	320 True pistachio
235	■	414 Dark steel
900	☐	648 Light beaver gray
885	☐	677 Pale old gold
140	☐	813 Medium powder blue
161	■	826 Bright blue
158	☐	828 Pale powder blue
1044	■	895 Dark hunter green
206	⊔	966 Baby green
268	◧	3345 Medium hunter green
266	⊻	3347 Medium yellow-green
862	☐	3348 Light yellow-green

BLENDED-NEEDLE HALF CROSS-STITCH
Stitch in this direction ╱

371 235	■	433 Dark chestnut (2X) and 414 Dark steel (1X)
370 235	☐	434 Medium chestnut (2X) and 414 Dark steel (1X)
1045 235	■	436 Dark tan (2X) and 414 Dark steel (1X)
900 391	☐	648 Light beaver gray (1X) and 3033 Pale mocha (2X)
874 885	☐	676 Light old gold (1X) and 677 Pale old gold (1X)
887	▷	739 Pale tan (2X) and 002 Kreinik Gold blending filament (1X)
1044	✻	895 Dark hunter green (2X) and 002 Kreinik Gold blending filament (1X)
386	☐	3823 Pale yellow (2X) and 091 Kreinik Star yellow blending filament (1X)

BACKSTITCH

332	╱	608 Orange – candle flame (2X)
380	╱	838 Beige-brown – face and hands on Santa and doll, beard and hair (1X)
1041	╱	844 Deep beaver gray – hammer head, floor line, walls, candle (1X); and Santa's glasses (2X)
382	╱	3371 Black-brown – all other stitches (1X)
	╱	202HL Kreinik Aztec gold #4 very-fine braid – buttons, doll's necklace (1X), sled runners (2X)

BLENDED-NEEDLE BACKSTITCH

590	╱	712 Cream (1X) and 002 Kreinik Gold blending filament (1X) – pipe smoke

STRAIGHT STITCH

382	╱	3371 Black-brown – horse's mane (1X)

FRENCH KNOT (1X wrapped twice)

382	●	3371 Black-brown – horse and doll eyes

Stitch count: 184 high x 120 wide

Finished design sizes:
28-count fabric – 13⅛ x 8½ inches
32-count fabric – 11½ x 7½ inches
36-count fabric – 10¼ x 6⅔ inches

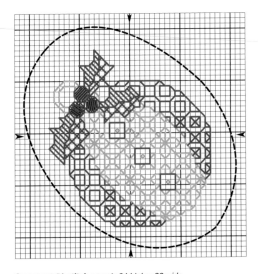

Ornament #1 stitch count: 34 high x 32 wide
Ornament #1 finished design sizes:
25-count fabric – 2¾ x 2½ inches
28-count fabric – 2⅜ x 2¼ inches
32-count fabric – 2⅛ x 2 inches

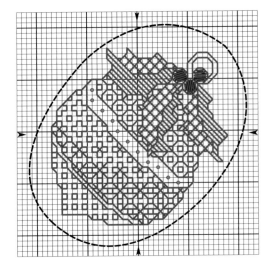

Ornament #2 stitch count: 34 high x 35 wide
Ornament #2 finished design sizes:
25-count fabric – 2¾ x 2⅞ inches
28-count fabric – 2⅜ x 2½ inches
32-count fabric – 2⅛ x 2¼ inches

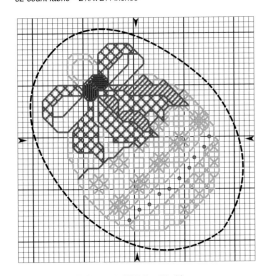

Ornament #3 stitch count: 36 high x 35 wide
Ornament #3 finished design sizes:
25-count fabric – 2⅞ x 2⅞ inches
28-count fabric – 2½ x 2½ inches
32-count fabric – 2¼ x 2¼ inches

½" beyond the edge of the board. Fold the edge of the fabric to the back and glue in place.

Cut a 13" length of the burgundy cord. Position and glue the cord around the edge of the ornament, overlapping the ends at the top center and trimming the excess.

For the hanger, cut a 6" length of burgundy cord. Fold the cord in half and glue the ends to the top center of the ornament back. Glue the felt to the back of the ornament.

Blackwork Ornaments

Anchor	DMC	

SATIN STITCH

| 1005 | 816 Garnet – holly berries (2X) |

BACKSTITCH

890	680 Old gold – blackwork design on ornaments 1 and 3 (1X), outline of ornament 1 and hanger on ornament 3 (2X)
923	699 Christmas green – blackwork design of leaves (1X), leaf outline (2X)
132	797 Royal blue – blackwork design on ornaments 1 and 2 (1X), outlines of ornaments 1 and 2 (2X)
1005	816 Garnet – blackwork design on ornament 1 (1X), holly berries, bow and outline of ornament 3, stripes on ornament 2 (2X)

MILL HILL BEADS

● 00020 Royal blue seed beads – ornament 2
○ 02011 Victorian gold seed beads – ornament 1
● 03049 Rich red seed beads – ornament 3

Blue Santa

Anchor	DMC
001	000 White
403	310 Black
979	312 Light navy
235	318 Steel
9046	321 Christmas red
146	322 Pale navy
150	336 Medium navy
9575	353 Dark peach
398	415 Pearl gray
371	433 Dark chestnut
370	434 Medium chestnut
297	444 Lemon
265	471 Avocado
046	666 Red
874	676 Light old gold
228	700 Medium Christmas green
239	702 Light Christmas green
257	703 Chartreuse
590	712 Cream
887	739 Tan
275	780 Topaz
307	783 Christmas gold
358	801 Coffee brown
390	822 Pale beige-gray
375	869 Hazel
152	939 Deep navy
1012	948 Light peach
039	961 Dark rose-pink
843	3012 Khaki
268	3345 Medium hunter green
267	3346 Light hunter green
025	3716 Light rose-pink
167	3766 Peacock blue
1009	3770 Ivory
901	3829 Deep old gold
1006	3831 Dark raspberry
028	3832 Medium raspberry
031	3833 Light raspberry
177	3838 Dark lavender-blue
120	3840 Light lavender-blue
002	3865 Winter white

BLENDED NEEDLE

370	434 Medium chestnut (1X) and
380	838 Deep beige-brown (1X)
392	642 Medium beige-gray (1X) and
390	822 Pale beige-gray (1X)
874	676 Light old gold (1X) and 002 Kreinik Gold blending filament (1X)

BACKSTITCH (1X)

403	310 Black – rocking horse halter
380	838 Deep beige-brown – Santa'a facial detail
379	840 Medium beige-brown – Santa's beard
382	3371 Black-brown – all other stitches
1006	3831 Dark raspberry – doll shoes
	221 Kreinik Antique gold #8 fine braid – soldier hat

STRAIGHT STITCH

001	000 White – eyebrows and eye detail (2X)
403	310 Black – rocking horse mane (2X)
9046	321 Christmas red – soldier hat feather (2X)
	003 Kreinik Red #32 braid – drum straps (1X)
	203 Kreinik Flame #8 fine braid – rocking horse (1X)
	221 Kreinik Antique gold #8 fine braid – drum detail (1X)

LAZY DAISY

| | 203 Kreinik Flame #8 fine braid – rocking horse (1X) |

FRENCH KNOT (1X wrapped twice)

| 382 | 3371 Black-brown – eyes on toys |

MILL HILL BEADS

○ 00557 Gold seed bead – drum, soldier hat
● 02013 Red red seed bead – Santa's cap
✕ 86346 Petite present button with 40161 crystal petite bead
✕ 86351 Petite gingerman button with 42013 red red petite bead

SURFACE ATTACHMENTS

003 Kreinik Red #32 braid – bow (1X)
● 6 mm gold jingle bells – ends of bow

Stitch count: 195 high x 127 wide
Finished design sizes:
32-count fabric – 12⅛ x 8 inches
28-count fabric – 14 x 9 inches
36-count fabric – 10⅞ x 7 inches

Christmas Past and Present

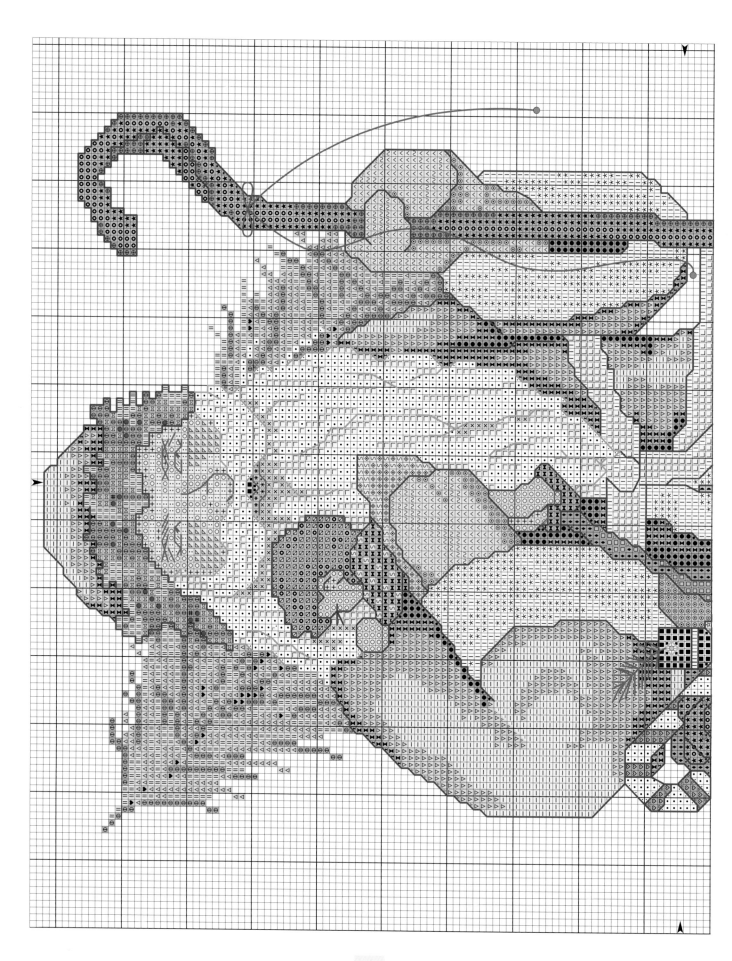

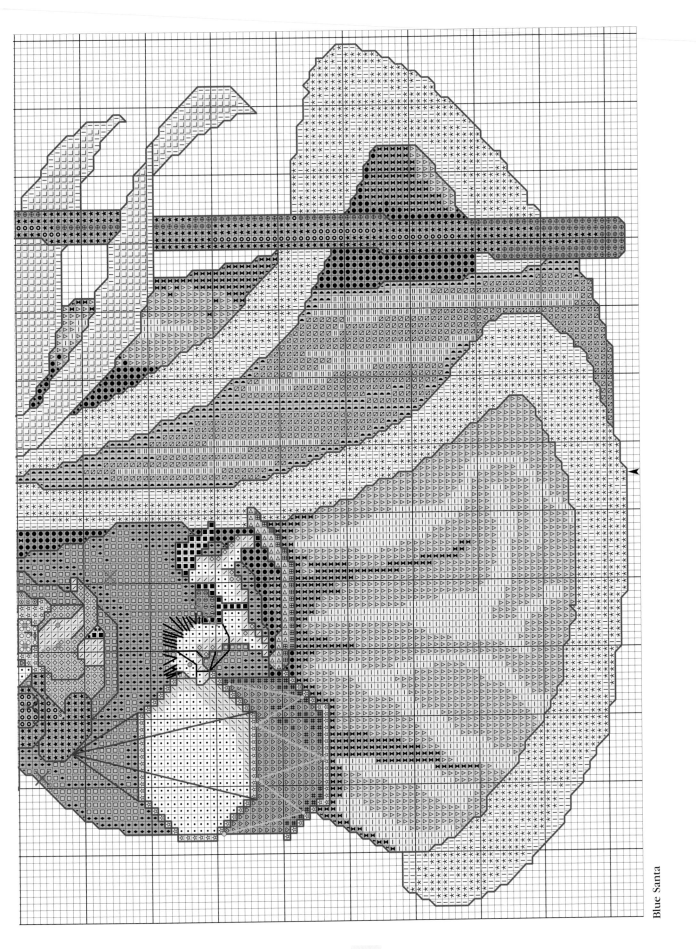

Blue Santa

Canaries and Pinecones

Christmas Past and Present

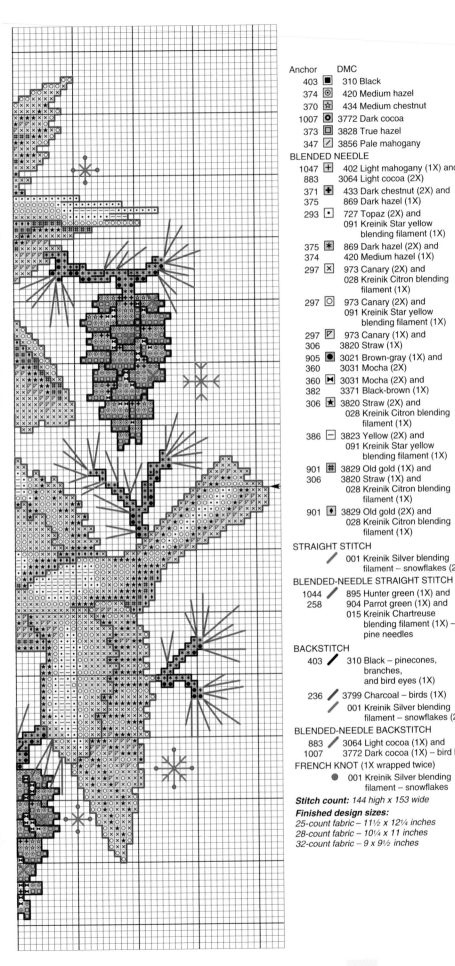

Anchor		DMC
403	■	310 Black
374	◉	420 Medium hazel
370	✿	434 Medium chestnut
1007	◉	3772 Dark cocoa
373	□	3828 True hazel
347	╱	3856 Pale mahogany

BLENDED NEEDLE

1047	✛	402 Light mahogany (1X) and
883		3064 Light cocoa (2X)
371	✚	433 Dark chestnut (2X) and
375		869 Dark hazel (1X)
293	·	727 Topaz (2X) and
		091 Kreinik Star yellow blending filament (1X)
375	✳	869 Dark hazel (2X) and
374		420 Medium hazel (1X)
297	✕	973 Canary (2X) and
		028 Kreinik Citron blending filament (1X)
297	○	973 Canary (2X) and
		091 Kreinik Star yellow blending filament (1X)
297	◸	973 Canary (1X) and
306		3820 Straw (1X)
905	●	3021 Brown-gray (1X) and
360		3031 Mocha (2X)
360	◰	3031 Mocha (2X) and
382		3371 Black-brown (1X)
306	★	3820 Straw (2X) and
		028 Kreinik Citron blending filament (1X)
386	⊟	3823 Yellow (2X) and
		091 Kreinik Star yellow blending filament (1X)
901	⊞	3829 Old gold (1X) and
306		3820 Straw (1X) and
		028 Kreinik Citron blending filament (1X)
901	◆	3829 Old gold (2X) and
		028 Kreinik Citron blending filament (1X)

STRAIGHT STITCH

	╱	001 Kreinik Silver blending filament – snowflakes (2X)

BLENDED-NEEDLE STRAIGHT STITCH

1044	╱	895 Hunter green (1X) and
258		904 Parrot green (1X) and
		015 Kreinik Chartreuse blending filament (1X) – pine needles

BACKSTITCH

403	╱	310 Black – pinecones, branches, and bird eyes (1X)
236	╱	3799 Charcoal – birds (1X)
	╱	001 Kreinik Silver blending filament – snowflakes (2X)

BLENDED-NEEDLE BACKSTITCH

883	╱	3064 Light cocoa (1X) and
1007		3772 Dark cocoa (1X) – bird legs

FRENCH KNOT (1X wrapped twice)

	●	001 Kreinik Silver blending filament – snowflakes

Stitch count: 144 high x 153 wide

Finished design sizes:
25-count fabric – 11½ x 12¼ inches
28-count fabric – 10¼ x 11 inches
32-count fabric – 9 x 9½ inches

Canaries and Pinecones

Supplies
18" square of 25-count Wedgwood
  Lugana fabric
Cotton embroidery floss
1 additional skein of straw (DMC
  3820); 2 additional skeins of canary
  (DMC 973) floss
Kreinik blending filament
1 additional spool of 028 citron
  blending filament
Desired frame

Stitches
Center and stitch the design on the
fabric. Use three plies of floss to work
the stitches over two threads of the
fabric unless otherwise specified.
Press the finished stitchery from the
back. Frame the piece as desired.

Canary Ornaments

Supplies
For each ornament
8" square of 36-count cream Edinburgh
  linen
Cotton embroidery floss
Kreinik blending filament
4" circle of self-stick mounting board
  with foam
4" circle of cream felt
6" length of ¼"-wide ivory satin ribbon
15½" length of ¼"-diameter ivory
  cording
Crafts glue

Stitches
Center and stitch the desired
individual canary motif on the linen.
Use two plies of floss to work the
stitches over two threads of the fabric
unless otherwise specified. Press the
stitchery from the back.

Assembly
Peel the protective paper from the
mounting board. Center the foam side
on the back of the stitchery and press
to stick. Trim the excess fabric
½" beyond the edge of the board.
Fold the edge of the fabric to the
back and glue in place.

Continued

Position and glue the cord around the edge of the ornament, overlapping the ends at the top center and trimming the excess.

For the hanger, fold the ivory ribbon in half to form a loop and glue the ends to the top center of the ornament back. Glue the felt to the back of the ornament.

Blue Santa

Supplies

15×20" piece of 32-count natural light linen
Cotton embroidery floss
Kreinik blending filament
Kreinik #8 fine braid
Kreinik #32 heavy braid
Mill Hill seed and petite seed beads
Mill Hill buttons
2—6mm gold jingle bells
Desired frame

Stitches

Center and stitch the design, *pages 21–23*, on the linen. Use two plies of floss to work the stitches over two threads of the fabric unless otherwise specified. Attach the seed beads using two plies of matching floss.

To attach the buttons, thread a beading needle with floss; knot the ends. Insert the needle through the fabric from back of the fabric at the position marked on the chart. Slip the button then a petite seed bead onto the needle. Push the needle back through the button and the fabric and secure it.

For Santa's staff ribbon, tie a bow in the center of a 20" length of red braid and tack it to the staff. Use a large tapestry needle to thread one end of the braid through the fabric to the back. Secure the end of the braid with matching floss. Repeat for the other braid end. On the front of the fabric, sew a jingle bell at each ribbon end. Press the stitchery facedown on a soft towel. Frame the piece as desired.

Green Santa

Supplies

15×20" piece of 32-count natural light linen
Cotton embroidery floss
Desired frame

Stitches

Center and stitch the design, *pages 27–29*, on the linen. Use two plies of floss to work the stitches over two threads of the fabric unless otherwise specified. Press from the back. Frame the piece as desired.

Monogram Stocking

Supplies

10" length of 18-count antique white petite fleur red-and-green Aida banding
Needle Necessities 8153 dazzling red overdyed #8 pearl cotton
8×12" piece of red rayon velvet
½ yard of red cotton fabric
8×12" piece of fleece
Rose rubber stamp
Spray bottle with water
Iron; ironing board

Use only rayon velvet for this project. The stamps will not imprint on any other type of velvet. Rubber stamps with intricate designs will not transfer well on the fabric.

Stitches

Chart the desired initials using the alphabets on *pages 30–31*. Center and stitch the initials on the banding. Use one strand of pearl cotton to work the stitches. Press the stitchery from the back. Set the cuff aside.

Assembly

Enlarge the stocking pattern, *above*. Use the pattern to cut the stocking front from the velvet.

Before printing the fabric, test the embossing method on a velvet scrap. To emboss the fabric, preheat the iron on the wool setting. Place the rubber stamp right side up on the ironing board. Spray the nap side of the velvet generously with water. Position the

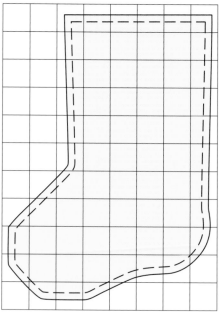

Monogram Stocking Pattern
1 square = 1"

velvet, nap side down, over the stamp and press firmly with the center of the iron for 20 seconds. Check the imprint, and if desired, press for an additional 10 seconds. Do not slide the iron over the rubber stamp—it will blur the image. Refer to the photograph on *page 15* to position the roses on the stocking.

Cut one stocking back, two lining pieces, and a 1⅝×5" hanging strip from the red cotton. Cut one interlining from the fleece.

Baste the fleece to the wrong side of the stocking front. With right sides together, sew the stocking front to the back with a ½" seam allowance, leaving the top edge open. Clip the curves and trim the seam allowance to ¼". Turn the stocking right side out and press carefully.

Press the long edges of the hanging strip under ¼"; fold the strip in half lengthwise, and topstitch. Fold the strip in half to form a loop. Tack the ends of the loop inside the top right side of the stocking.

Sew the lining pieces together, with right sides together, leaving the top edge open and an opening in the foot; *do not* turn.

Slip the stocking inside the lining. Stitch the stocking to the lining at the top edges with right sides together;

turn. Slip-stitch the opening closed. Tuck the lining into the stocking and press carefully.

Measure the distance around the top of the stocking and add 1". Trim the banding to this length. Overcast the banding's cut edges to prevent fraying, then sew them together using a ½" seam. Slip the banding over the stocking top; slip-stitch in place.

Monogram Brooch

Supplies
4" square of 32-count English mist linen

Antique violet cotton embroidery floss (DMC 3041)

Purchased 1⅝×¹³⁄₁₆" oval brooch (Mill Hill AG3)

Stitches
Center and stitch the desired large initial, *page 31,* on the linen. Use one ply of floss to work the stitches over one thread of the fabric. Press the stitchery from the back. Insert the fabric into the brooch following the manufacturer's instructions.

Monogram Sachet

Supplies
2—6" squares of 32-count cherub pink linen

Shell pink cotton embroidery floss (DMC 223)

Polyester fiberfill

Potpourri (optional)

7½" length of 1¾"-wide ecru flat lace

½ yard of ¼"-wide rose satin ribbon

Purchased 3"-long rose tassel

Stitches
Chart the desired initials using the alphabets on *pages 30–31.* Center and stitch the initials on the linen. Use two plies of floss to work the cross-stitches over two threads of the fabric. Work the backstitches using one ply. Press the stitchery from the back.

Assembly
Centering the design, and with a corner at the top, draw a 3¾" square

on the fabric; cut out on traced line. Cut a matching back from the remaining piece of linen.

Fold the short ends of the lace under ¼". With raw edges together, baste the lace to the right side of the bottom of the stitched square, keeping the ends ¼" from adjacent corners and easing as needed.

With right sides facing, sew the sachet front and back together, leaving an opening for turning. Clip the

corners, turn the sachet right side out, and press. Stuff firmly with polyester fiberfill. If desired insert potpourri in the center of the stuffing. Slip-stitch the opening closed.

For the hanger, sew a 9" length of ribbon to the sides of sachet front 2¼" from the top point. Cut the remaining ribbon into two equal lengths; tie the pieces into bows. Tack the bows over the ends of the hanger. Sew the tassel to the bottom behind the lace.

Green Santa

Anchor		DMC
001	⊡	000 White
1006	⊠	304 Medium Christmas red
218	⊞	319 Dark pistachio
9046	⊛	321 True Christmas red
5975	⊙	356 Medium terra-cotta
235	✳	414 Steel
398	⠒	415 Light pearl gray
371	▲	433 Dark chestnut
1046	◯	435 Light chestnut
362	⌃	437 Tan
1005	◉	498 Dark Christmas red
979	◆	517 Wedgwood blue
046	◈	666 Red
874	▢	676 Light old gold
885	▯	677 Pale old gold
227	☆	701 True Christmas green
239	⦀	702 Light Christmas green
257	⟋	703 Chartreuse
890	⋈	729 Medium old gold
303	△	742 Tangerine
302	⌐	743 True yellow
301	⊕	744 Medium yellow
868	◺	754 Peach
1022	✶	760 True salmon
1021	⌊	761 Light salmon
234	▽	762 Pale pearl gray
308	◩	782 Topaz

307	⍁	783 Christmas gold
390	S	822 Beige-gray
379	⌐	840 Medium beige-brown
376	⋁	842 Light beige-brown
683	●	890 Deep pistachio
882	▽	945 Dark ivory
1010	⊞	951 Medium ivory
246	✚	986 Dark forest green
244	⏀	987 Medium forest green
382	■	3371 Black-brown
1013	⊠	3778 True terra-cotta
306	▷	3820 Dark straw
891	◥	3822 Light straw
339	⊞	3830 Terra-cotta
897	⋈	3857 Dark rosewood
896	⋂	3858 Medium rosewood
1007	≡	3859 Light rosewood
906	▣	3862 Dark mocha-beige
378	◿	3864 Light mocha-beige
002	⊟	3865 Winter white
926	⌁	3866 Mocha
	▷	003HL Kreinik Red high luster blending filament

BLENDED NEEDLE

9046	♡	321 True Christmas red (1X) and 003HL Kreinik Red high luster blending filament (1X)
1005	★	498 Dark Christmas red (1X) and 003HL Kreinik Red high luster blending filament (1X)
683	⊠	890 Deep pistachio (1X) and 008HL Kreinik Green high luster blending filament (1X)

BACKSTITCH

001	╱	000 White – eyebrows (2X), eye highlights (1X)
358	╱	801 Coffee brown – bottom of gown (1X)
380	╱	838 Deep beige-brown – Santa's bag and eyes (1X)
379	╱	840 Medium beige-brown – Santa's face, beard and hair (1X)
382	╱	3371 Black-brown – all other stitches (1X)

Stitch count: *192 high x 112 wide*

Finished design sizes:
32-count fabric – 12 x 7 inches
28-count fabric – 13¾ x 8 inches
36-count fabric – 10⅔ x 6¼ inches

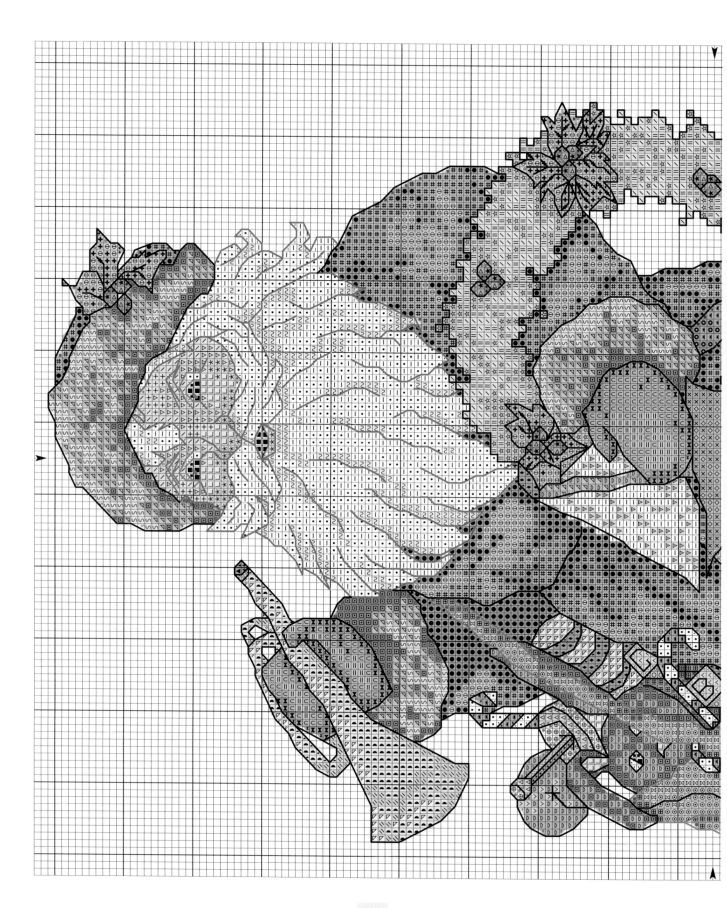

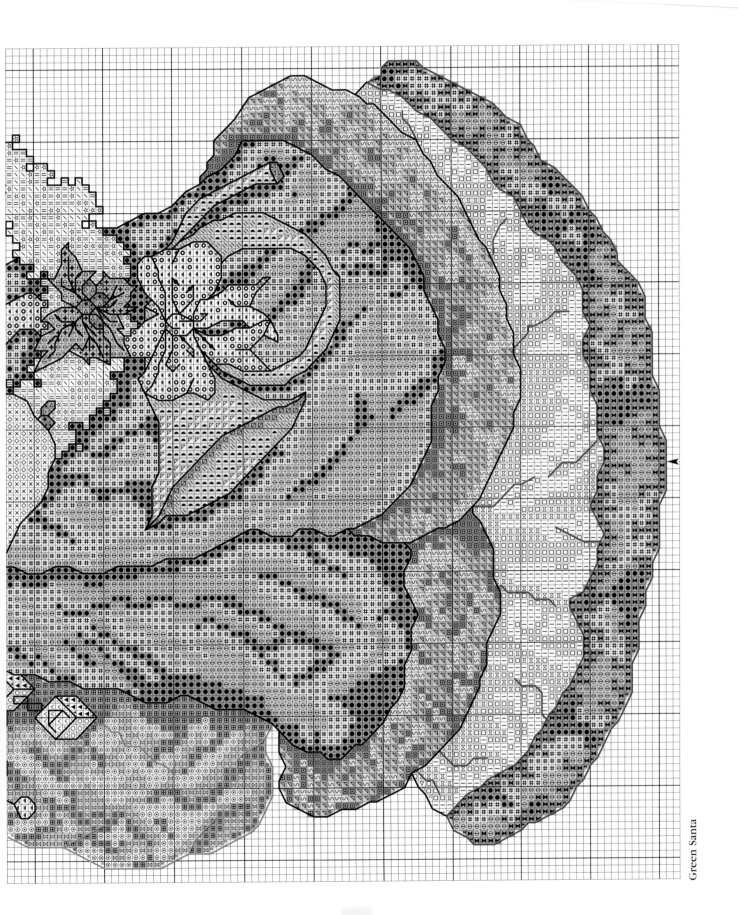

Monogram Purse

Supplies

2—6" squares of 32-count bonnie
  blue linen
Deep gray-blue (DMC 924) and dark
  gray-blue (DMC 3768) cotton
  embroidery floss
6×8" piece of cream lining fabric
Purchased 2"-wide silver purse frame
  (Lacis #LS69)
2 silver split rings
16"-long silver chain

Stitches

Center and stitch the desired large
initial on one piece of the linen. Use
two plies of dark gray-blue floss to
work the cross-stitches over two
threads of the fabric. Work the

backstitches
using one ply of
deep gray-blue
floss. Press the
stitchery from
the back.

Assembly

Transfer the
purse pattern,
below, onto the
tracing paper;
cut out. Center
the pattern on
the stitchery and
cut out. Cut a
back from the
remaining linen
and two lining pieces from the
cream fabric.

Using a ¼" seam allowance, sew
the purse front and back together,
right sides facing, between the dots
indicated on the pattern. Turn right
side out; press. Sew the lining pieces
together in the same manner; *do not*
turn; set aside.

Cut two 14" lengths of deep
gray-blue floss (DMC 924).
Combine the plies into a single 12-ply strand. Secure one
end of the joined strands and
twist until tightly wound.
Holding the ends, fold the
strand in half as the two
halves twist around each
other. Slip-stitch the twisted

Monogram Small Alphabet

cord to the seam of the purse, tucking
the cord ends inside the purse at the
seam ends.

Press the top edges of the purse
and lining under ⅛". Slip the lining
into the purse, matching side seams.
Baste the folded edges of the purse
and lining together.

Open the purse frame. Matching the
seams with the joints of the frame,
position the purse in the frame and
baste loosely. Working from the inside
of the frame, carefully sew through
the fabric, into an opening in the
frame, and back into the fabric.
Continue sewing around both sides of
the frame ending at the starting point.
Remove the basting threads. Attach
the chain using the split rings.

Monogram Purse Diagram

Monogram Large Alphabet

*M*onogram Book Cover
Fits a book up to 8×6".

Supplies
*16×22" piece of 28-count friendship
    blue linen
Gold cotton embroidery floss
    (DMC 676)
7×11" piece of fusible fleece
¾ yard of ⅜"-wide blue ribbon
1 yard of ⅛"-diameter gold-and-cream
    sew-in cording
Book
Erasable fabric marking pen*

Stitches
Chart the desired initials using the
alphabets. Cut a 9×16" rectangle from
the linen. Use basting thread to divide
the piece into two 9×8" sections.
Center and stitch the monogram on
the right section of the linen. Work
the backstitches first using one ply of
floss. Then use three plies of floss to
fill the spaces between the
backstitches with satin stitches. Press
the stitchery from the back.

Assembly
Make a pattern for the book cover by
tracing around the open book on
tracing paper, marking the position of
the spine; cut out ¼"
beyond the outline.
Pin the pattern to
the stitchery with the
monogram centered on
the book front;
cut out.

Use the pattern to
cut an interlining from
the fleece and a lining
from the linen. Also
cut two pocket flaps,
the height of the
pattern and 3¾" wide,
from the linen.

Fuse the fleece to the
back of the book cover
following the
manufacturer's
instructions. Sew the
piping around the
perimeter of the book
cover with raw edges
even, overlapping
the ends.

Fold the ribbon in half and sew the
folded edge to the top center of the
book cover.

Press one long edge of each pocket
flap under ¼" twice; topstitch. With
right sides together, sew the top and
bottom and the unpressed long edge
of one flap to one short end of the
cover. Clip the corners, but *do not*
turn. Repeat for the other flap.

With right sides together, sew the
lining and the cover together along
the long edges to form a tube. Turn
the tube right side out, and press.
Insert the ends of the book into the
pocket ends.

*L*et the light
side of Christmas
inspire your

holiday spirits—and

your decor. Stitch up

some whimsy to

scatter throughout the

house and to give

as gifts.

High-Spirited Holidays

*B*righten *your walls with a Christmas alphabet.*

There's a familiar holiday symbol for every letter of the alphabet. Stitch the entire banner
on 18-count Aida cloth or select your favorite letters to stitch as ornaments. You'll find dozens
of uses for a holiday-color patchwork tote bag that features the cheery Merry Christmas
motif, stitched on 11-count Aida.

Design: Christmas Alphabet, Barbara Sestok

*I*f you believe there's magic in Christmas, say it in cross-stitch!
*The framed sampler, stitched on 14-count Aida cloth, brings holiday cheer to almost any room of
the house. Use the individual motifs and designs for ornaments, package ties, or trim on holiday
napkin rings and napkins stitched on 14-count Vienna fabric.*

Design: Believe in the Magic, Williams Wonder Works

$\mathcal{E}$*nhance a Santa collection with a banner featuring a festive trio*
of old-world gift givers. Stitch it on 26-count Heatherfield and finish with a border of colorful
patchwork and a faux pepper-berry hanger. Or, enlarge a Santa collection with any
one of the three figures stitched on 10-count Tula fabric and stuffed.
By interchanging the red-coat and the green-mitten colors, the central figure of the wall
hanging takes on very different looks.

Design: I Love Santa, Robin Clark

Welcome the newest member of the family
with a sweet teddy bear stocking. Worked on creamy wool
Aida cloth with soft pastels, it's a first Christmas gift that baby will
appreciate for years. There's an alternate color key if you prefer
the bear's cap and bow in baby blue.

A touch of whimsy spreads the merriment of the holiday.
This perky hen on her basket of ornament eggs is a natural for the kitchen. Stitch her
alone, then frame her with colorful fabric for a holiday trivet.

Designs: Baby Stocking, Lorrie Birmingham; Hatching Christmas Cheer, De Selby

*H*oe! Hoe! Hoe! Santa decked in gardening gear is sure to please
the cultivator in your life. This special stocking has lots of pretty border motifs to plant
on smaller projects, such as a band for a broad-brimmed garden hat.

Design: Hoe! Hoe! Hoe! Robin Clark

Christmas Alphabet Banner

Anchor		DMC	
002	•	000	White
290	⊙	307	True lemon
403	■	310	Black
235	⏀	318	Steel
218	▲	319	Pistachio
914	◗	407	Cocoa
398	S	415	Pearl gray
1046	▽	435	Chestnut
288	✳	445	Light lemon
098	◗	553	Violet
266	⌗	581	True moss green
874	L	676	Light old gold
228	✕	700	Medium Christmas green
239	○	702	Light Christmas green
256	⊐	704	Chartreuse
304	≡	741	Tangerine
868	I	754	Peach
159	∶	775	Baby blue
275	⊕	780	Topaz
132	◆	797	Royal blue
045	♥	814	Dark garnet
1005	⊞	816	Light garnet
227	✚	911	Emerald
204	△	913	Nile green
026	♡	957	Geranium
187	∼	958	True aqua
186	∧	959	Medium aqua
1070	+	964	Light aqua
297	☆	973	Canary
1001	◇	976	Golden brown
281	‖	3011	Khaki
025	▨	3716	Rose-pink
236	●	3799	Charcoal
279	−	3819	Light moss green
306	⋈	3820	Dark straw
305	╱	3821	True straw
313	□	3825	Bittersweet
373	✳	3828	Hazel
901	★	3829	Deep old gold
1006	◆	3831	Dark raspberry
028	k	3832	Medium raspberry
100	∩	3837	Lavender
177	▼	3838	Dark lavender-blue
176	⌂	3839	Medium lavender-blue
1074	⧄	3848	Teal green
311	∨	3855	Autumn gold
896	U	3858	Medium rosewood
1007	▷	3859	Light rosewood
906	◈	3862	Dark mocha-beige
001	⍂	3865	Winter white
926	⌧	3866	Pale mocha-beige

Continued

Christmas Alphabet Banner—Top

Christmas Alphabet Banner

BACKSTITCH

403	╱	310 Black – all other stitches (1X)
403	╱	310 Black – light cord (2X),
297	╱	973 Canary – gingerman vest (2X)

STRAIGHT STITCH

403	╱	310 Black – details on elf and gingerman (1X)
297	╱	973 Canary – bell clapper and package bow on letter "E" (2X)

LAZY DAISY

297	◊	973 Canary – package bow on letter "E" (2X)

FRENCH KNOT

403	●	310 Black – angel on letter "A", King on letter "K" and Santa eyes on letter "V" (1X wrapped once)
403	●	310 Black – nutcracker on letter "N", elf on letter "E", gingerman on letter "G" and bear eyes on letter "U" (2X wrapped once)
228	●	700 Medium Christmas green – reindeer collar (2X wrapped twice)
297	○	973 Canary – center of package bow on letter "E" (1X wrapped twice)
1006	●	3831 Dark raspberry – fireplace trim, king's crown, train wheels on the letter "U" (2X wrapped once)

Stitch count: 272 high x 155 wide

Finished design sizes:
18-count fabric – 15⅛ x 8⅝ inches
16-count fabric – 17 x 9⅝ inches
14-count fabric – 19⅜ x 11 inches

Christmas Alphabet Banner

Supplies

18×24" piece of 18-count white Aida cloth
Cotton embroidery floss
1 additional skein each of white and chartreuse (DMC 704) floss
2 additional skeins each of black (DMC 310) and bittersweet (DMC 3825) floss
⅛ yard of 45"-wide blue print fabric
10½×16½" piece of quilt batting
10½×16½" piece of white cotton fabric
11½" length of ¼"-diameter wooden dowel
2—½×⅝" wooden candle cups
Blue acrylic paint
1 yard of ⅝"-wide red satin ribbon

Continued

Christmas Alphabet Banner—Bottom

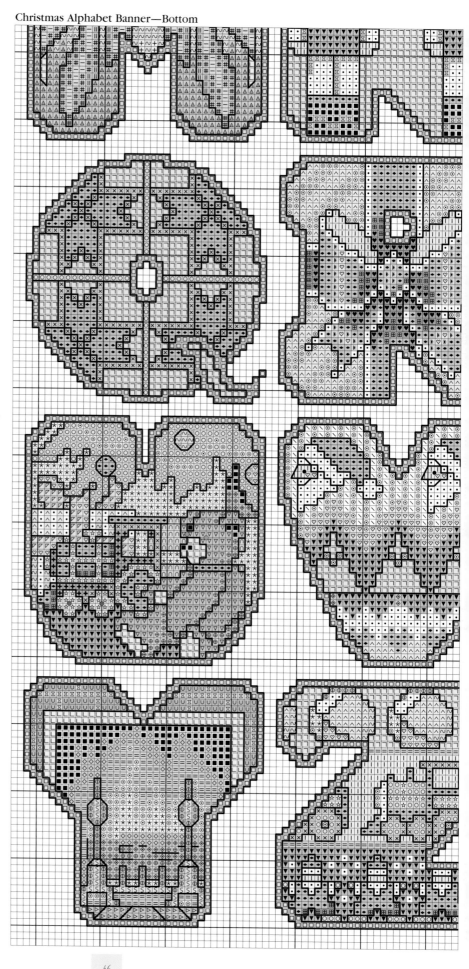

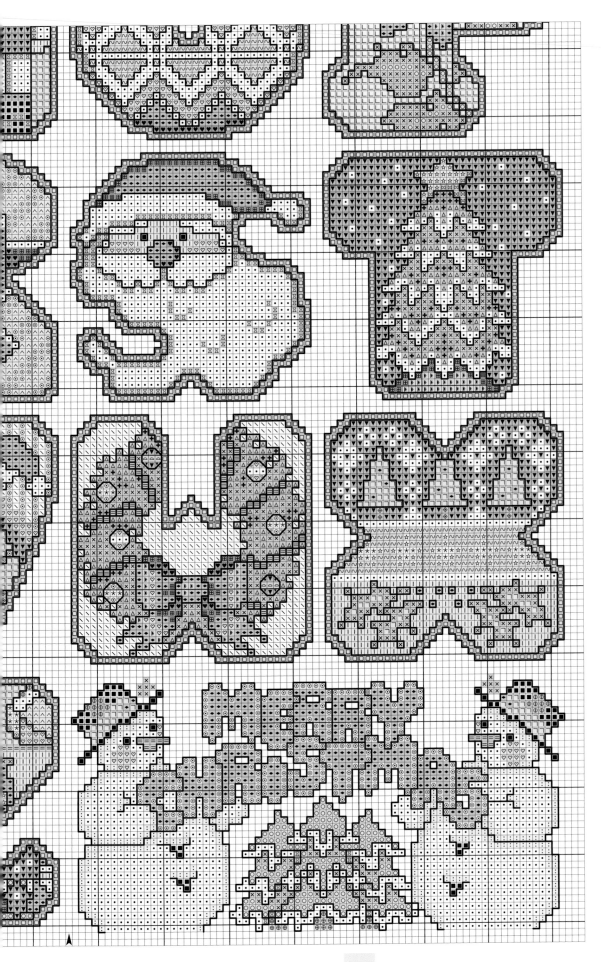

High-Spirited Holidays

Stitches

Center and stitch the design, *pages 44–47,* on the fabric. Use two plies of floss to work the stitches unless otherwise specified. Press the stitchery from the back. Centering the design, trim the stitchery to measure 10×16".

Assembly

From the blue-print fabric, cut a 10×16" back and a 5×9" strip for the rod pocket. Cut and join strips of the blue fabric to make a 2½×50" binding strip. Set the pieces aside. (All measurements given include ¼" seam allowances unless otherwise specified in the instructions.)

Place the quilt back, wrong side facing up, on a smooth surface. Center and smooth the quilt batting on top of the back. Center the stitched piece atop the batting and baste all layers together. With right sides facing, fold the rod-pocket strip in half lengthwise. Sew across both short ends. Turn right side out and press. Baste the rod pocket to the back of the wall hanging with the raw edges even with the top. Hand-stitch the folded edge of the rod pocket to the back of the wall hanging, leaving the ends open.

Fold the binding strip in half lengthwise and press. Pin the binding to the banner, right sides together. Stitch through all layers, mitering corners. Turn the binding to the back of the banner and blindstitch in place.

Press a candle cup onto each end of the ¼" dowel. Paint the rod and candle cups with blue acrylic paint. Allow to dry. Slip the dowel into the rod pocket of the banner. Cut a 24" piece of ribbon and tie each end around a candle cup, leaving a 4" tail. Tie the remaining ribbon around the hanger and into a bow. Trim all the ribbon ends diagonally.

Christmas Alphabet Ornaments

Supplies

For each ornament
7" square of 18-count white Aida cloth
Cotton embroidery floss
7×15" piece of a coordinating print
    cotton fabric

Stitches

Center and stitch the desired letter from the chart, *pages 44–47,* on the Aida cloth. Use two plies of floss to work the cross-stitches. Work the backstitches using one ply. Press from the back.

Assembly

Centering the design, trim the stitchery to a 4" square. Cut a 4"-square back and two 4"-square lining pieces from the print fabric.

For the hanger, cut six 36"-long six-ply lengths of two different floss colors. Combine the cut lengths into one strand. Twist the strand until it begins to kink up on itself. Holding the ends with your fingers, fold the strand in half and the two strands will twist around each other. Glue the unfinished end to secure it.

Tuck the ends of the twisted cord to the between the ornament front and back ½" from the bottom edge.

Sew the ornament front and back together along the sides and bottom using ½" seams, leaving the top edge unstitched and taking care to catch only the ends of the twisted cord; turn right side out. Sew the lining pieces together in the same manner, leaving an opening in one side for turning; *do not* turn.

Slip the ornament inside the lining with the seams matching and raw edges even. Sew around the top edges; turn right side out through the opening in the lining. Slip-stitch the opening closed. Tuck the lining into the ornament and press carefully. Hand stitch the twisted cord to the sides of the ornament.

Merry Christmas Tote

Supplies

10×14" piece of 11-count white
    Aida cloth
Cotton embroidery floss
⅛ yard of 45"-wide red print fabric
⅝ yard of 45"-wide pale blue fabric
⅝ yard of 45"-wide green print fabric
2—17½×15½" pieces of fusible fleece

Stitches

Center and stitch the Merry Christmas motif from the alphabet chart, *page 47,* on the Aida cloth. Use four plies of floss to work the cross-stitches. Work the remaining stitches as specified. Press the stitchery from the back. Centering the design, trim the stitchery to a 5¼×8¼" rectangle.

Assembly

From the red print fabric, cut two 1½×8¼" top and bottom sashing strips, two 1½×7" side sashing strips, and two 1¾×19" handles. (All measurements given include ¼" seam allowances unless otherwise specified in the instructions.)

From the pale blue fabric, cut two 2×10¼" top and bottom sashing strips, two 2×10¼" side sashing strips, and two 17½×15½" lining pieces.

From the green print fabric, cut one 2¾×13¼" top sashing strip, one 3¾×13¼" bottom sashing strips, two 2¼×15½" side sashing strips, one 17½×15½" back, and two 1¾×19" handles.

Sew a red sashing strip to the top and bottom of the stitched piece. Sew a red side sashing strip to each side of the stitched piece.

Sew a pale blue sashing strip to the top and bottom of the stitchery. Sew a pale blue side sashing strip to each side of the stitchery.

Sew a green sashing strip to the top and bottom of the stitchery. Sew a green side sashing strip to each side of the stitchery.

Fuse the fleece to the back of the bag front and back pieces following

Continued

High-Spirited Holidays

the manufacturer's instructions. Sew the bag front to the back, right sides together, using ½" seams. Turn right side out and press.

Sew the long edges of one red and one green handle together. Turn right side out and press. With raw edges even, stitch the ends of one handle to the bag front 4½" from the side seams; baste. Repeat for the back handle.

Sew the lining pieces together in the same manner as the front, leaving an opening for turning in one side; *do not* turn. Slip the tote inside the lining. Stitch the tote to the lining at the top with right sides together and using ½" seam allowances; turn. Slip-stitch the opening closed. Tuck the lining into the tote. Machine topstitch around the top of the tote ¼" from the edge.

Believe in the Magic Sampler

Supplies
18×14" piece of 14-count white
*   Aida cloth*
Cotton embroidery floss

1 additional skein each of garnet
*   (DMC 815) and true emerald (DMC*
*   910) floss*
Desired frame

Stitches
Center and stitch the design, *pages 52–53,* on the fabric. Use three plies of floss to work the stitches unless otherwise specified. Attach beads using matching floss. Press the finished stitchery from the back. Frame the piece as desired.

Christmas Light Napkins

Supplies
For each napkin
15" square of 21-count white
*   Vienna fabric*
Cotton embroidery floss

Stitches
Fold the edges of the fabric under ½" twice on all four sides; topstitch. Measure ½" from the edges on one corner of the fabric; begin stitching the napkin chart there. Use three plies of floss to work the stitches unless otherwise specified; press.

Christmas Light Napkin Rings

Supplies
For each napkin ring
5×10" piece of 21-count white
*   Vienna fabric*
Cotton embroidery floss
15" length of purchased ⅛"-diameter
*   red sew-in piping*
2×6⅞" piece of white cotton fabric

Stitches
Center and stitch the design on the fabric. Use three plies of floss to work the stitches unless otherwise specified. Press from the back.

Assembly
Centering the design, trim the fabric to measure 2×6⅞." (All measurements given include ¼" seam allowances.) Cut the piping in half and sew one piece to each long edge of the stitchery with raw edges even. Place the 2×6⅞" piece of white cotton fabric and the stitchery with right sides together and raw edges aligned. Use a zipper foot to machine-stitch along the long edges. Trim the seams, turn right side out, and press.

Press one raw short end of the fabric under ¼". Tuck the other short end into the opening formed to over-lap the fabric. Hand-stitch the fabric together to form a ring.

Believe In The Magic

Anchor		DMC	
9046	◇	321	Christmas red
316	☆	740	Tangerine
302	=	743	Yellow
161	△	826	Bright blue
146	~	827	Powder blue
1098	⊕	3801	Watermelon
923	◉	3818	Deep emerald

BACKSTITCH (1X)

316	/	740	Tangerine – orange lights
043	/	815	Garnet – red lights
161	/	826	Bright blue – blue lights
923	/	3818	Deep emerald – light sockets

Napkin stitch count: *28 high x 34 wide*

Napkin finished design sizes:
21-count fabric – 2⅔ x 3¼ inches
28-count fabric – 2 x 2⅜ inches
25-count fabric – 2¼ x 2¾ inches

Believe In The Magic Napkin

Napkin Ring stitch count: *8 high x 61 wide*
Napkin Ring finished design sizes:
21-count fabric – ¾ x 5⅞ inches
28-count fabric – ½ x 4⅓ inches
25-count fabric – ⅝ x 4⅞ inches

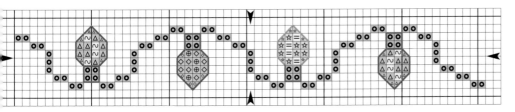

Believe In The Magic Napkin Ring

Believe in the Magic

Anchor		DMC	
002	•	000	White
403	■	310	Black
9046	◇	321	Christmas red
9575	▷	353	Dark peach
885	—	677	Old gold
316	☆	740	Tangerine
302	‖	743	Yellow
234	◁	762	Pearl gray
275	◆	780	Deep topaz
309	#	781	Dark topaz
307	○	783	Christmas gold
043	▶	815	Garnet

161	◿	826	Bright blue
146	2	827	Powder blue
228	✕	910	True emerald
1012	⟋	948	Light peach
1098	⊙	3801	Watermelon
923	⊡	3818	Deep emerald
	⠒	5282	Metallic gold

BACKSTITCH (1X)

403		310	Black — all other stitches
316		740	Tangerine — orange lights
043		815	Garnet — red lights, poinsettias, and lettering

| 161 | ╱ | 826 | Bright blue – blue lights |
| 923 | ╱ | 3818 | Deep emerald – leaves, holly, bells, year, and light sockets |

FRENCH KNOT

| 403 | ● | 310 | Black — eyes (2X wrapped once) |

MILL HILL BEADS

●		00557	Gold seed beads – poinsettia centers, toes of elf shoes, and elf hats
●		02013	Red red seed beads – holly berries, elves, and reindeer
●		02014	Black seed beads – reindeer nose, buttons on snowman, elves' clothing, and Mr. and Mrs. Santa's clothing

Stitch count: 180 high x 111 wide

Finished design sizes:
14-count fabric – 12⅞ x 8 inches
16-count fabric – 11¼ x 7 inches
18-count fabric – 10 x 6⅛ inches

High-Spirited Holidays

With raw edges even and right sides facing, sew one 11-square pieced strip to the left side of the stitchery. Sew the matching strip to the right side. Sew the remaining pieced strips to the top and bottom of the stitchery. Press the seams toward the borders.

Place the quilt back, wrong side up, on a smooth surface. Center and smooth the quilt batting on top. Center the stitchery atop the batting and baste all layers together. Machine-stitch in the ditch along the edges of the pieced border. Trim the back and batting even with the front.

Pin the binding to the banner, right sides together. Stitch through all layers, and miter corners. Turn the binding to the back of the banner and turn under ¼" along raw edges. Blindstitch in place.

I Love Santa Banner

Supplies

16×18" piece of 26-count white birch Heatherfield fabric
Cotton embroidery floss
⅜ yard of 45"-wide green-and-black check fabric
⅛ yard each of 45"-wide green-print fabric and burgundy-print fabric
12×14" piece of quilt batting

Stitches

Center and stitch the design on the fabric. Use three plies of floss to work the stitches over two threads of the fabric unless otherwise specified. Press the stitchery from the back. Centering the design, trim the stitchery to measure 9½×11½".

Assembly

From the green check fabric, cut a 12×14" back and enough 2"-wide bias strips to make a 52" binding strip. (All measurements given include ¼" seam allowances.)

From the green print, cut eleven 1½×4" strips; repeat with the burgundy print. Alternating colors, sew 11 strips together lengthwise. Repeat with the remaining strips. (One pieced strip will have green print at each end; the other will have burgundy print at each end.) From each pieced strip, cut two 1½"-wide segments.

I Love Santa Banner

Anchor		DMC	
002	•	000	White
897	◓	221	Deep shell pink
895	☆	223	Medium shell pink
403	■	310	Black
218	▢	319	Pistachio
1025	✕	347	Salmon
1014	◆	355	Dark terra-cotta
5975	▤	356	Medium terra-cotta
853	▥	372	Pecan
683	●	500	Deep blue-green
878	✳	501	Dark blue-green
853	△	613	Drab brown
874	✚	676	Old gold
9575	♡	758	Light terra-cotta
045	♥	902	Garnet
1035	◉	930	Antique blue
862	★	934	Pine green
4146	⁄	950	Rose-beige
905	▲	3021	Deep brown-gray
040	▬	3023	Light brown-gray
903	◈	3032	Medium mocha
262	⊡	3052	Gray-green
1015	✚	3777	Deep terra-cotta
1013	⊘	3778	True terra-cotta
1050	▦	3781	Dark mocha

BACKSTITCH
897	╱	221	Deep shell pink – mouths on toys (1X)
403	╱	310	Black – bridle on rocking horse (1X)
218	╱	319	Pistachio – hat detail on Santa #2 and sheep pull toy collar (3X)
905	╱	3021	Deep brown-gray – branches in arm of Santa #3 (3X), all other stitches (1X)

STRAIGHT STITCH
| 002 | ╱ | 000 | White – eyebrows (2X), moustaches (4X) |

COUCHING
| 218 | ╱ | 319 | Pistachio – ribbon on staff of Santa #1 (3X with 1X of same) |

FRENCH KNOT
| 1014 | ● | 355 | Dark terra-cotta – corners of mouths (1X wrapped once) |
| 905 | ● | 3021 | Deep brown-gray – wheels on sheep pull toy, all eyes (1X wrapped twice) |

Stitch count: *133 high x 107 wide*
Finished design sizes:
26-count fabric – 10¼ x 8¼ inches
28-count fabric – 9½ x 7⅝ inches
32-count fabric – 8⅓ x 6⅔ inches

I Love Santa Figure

Anchor		DMC	
002	•	000	White
897	✳	221	Deep shell pink
895	☆	223	Medium shell pink
403	■	310	Black
683	◓	500	Deep blue-green
878	♥	501	Dark blue-green
853	△	613	Drab brown
874	✚	676	Old gold
9575	♡	758	Light terra-cotta
045	●	902	Garnet
1035	◉	930	Antique blue
4146	⁄	950	Rose-beige
905	▲	3021	Deep brown-gray
903	◈	3032	Medium mocha
1013	⊘	3778	True terra-cotta
1050	▦	3781	Dark mocha

BACKSTITCH
897	╱	221	Deep shell pink – mouths on toys (2X)
403	╱	310	Black – bridle on rocking horse (1X)
218	╱	319	Pistachio – hat detail on Santa #2 and sheep pull toy collar (3X)
905	╱	3021	Deep brown-gray – all other stitches (2X)

STRAIGHT STITCH
| 002 | ╱ | 000 | White – eyebrows (2X), moustaches (4X) |

FRENCH KNOT
| 1014 | ● | 355 | Dark terra-cotta – corners of mouths (1X wrapped once) |
| 905 | ● | 3021 | Deep brown-gray – wheels on sheep pull toy, all eyes (1X wrapped twice) |

I Love Santa

I Love Santa Figure

Supplies
10×14" piece of 10-count cream
   Tula fabric
Cotton embroidery floss
⅛ yard of 45"-wide green cotton fabric
5×10" piece of fusible fleece
19" length of ⅛"-diameter cording
2½" circle of cardboard
Erasable fabric marking pen
Polyester fiberfill
Plastic pellets

Stitches
Center and stitch the center Santa from the chart, *page 55*, on the fabric. Use four plies of floss to work the cross-stitches. Work the backstitches using two plies. Work the remaining stitches as specified in the key. Press the stitchery from the back.

Assembly
Center and fuse the fleece to the wrong side of the stitchery following the manufacturer's instructions. Use the erasable marking pen to draw an outline ½" beyond the outermost stitched areas. Cut out the shape ½" beyond the traced line.

Use the stitched piece as a pattern to cut a matching back from the green fabric. Also cut a 1×19" piping strip from the green fabric.

Center the cording lengthwise on the wrong side of the piping strip. Fold the fabric over the cording, with the long edges together. Using a zipper foot, sew close to the cording

through all layers. Sew the piping around the perimeter of the figure with raw edges even.

With right sides facing, sew the front and back together, leaving the bottom edge open. Trim the seams, clip the curves, and turn right side out.

For the base, draw around the cardboard circle on the green fabric. Cut out ½" beyond the traced line. Center and glue the cardboard to the back of the green fabric. Fold the raw edges to the back and glue, clipping as needed. Let the glue dry.

Stuff the figure firmly with fiberfill, leaving the bottom 2" unstuffed. Fill a sandwich bag with plastic pellets; seal. Insert the bag into the bottom of the figure. Add fiberfill around the bag until the figure is firm. Fold the bottom edge of the figure under ½". Hand-stitch the base to the bottom of the figure.

Hatching Christmas Cheer Sampler

Supplies
10×16" piece of 14-count white
   Aida cloth
Cotton embroidery floss

Stitches
Center and stitch the design on the fabric. Use three plies of floss to work the stitches unless otherwise specified. Press the finished stitchery from the back. Frame the piece as desired.

Hen Trivet

Supplies
9×10" piece of 18-count white
   Aida cloth
Cotton embroidery floss
¼ yard of 45"-wide red cotton fabric
4" square of green cotton fabric
2—7×8" pieces of heavy fleece

Stitches
Center and stitch the hen motif from the chart on the fabric. Use two plies of floss to work the stitches unless otherwise specified. Press the stitchery from the back. Centering the design, trim the stitchery to a 6×7" rectangle.

Assembly
From the red fabric, cut a 7×8" back, two 2×6" top and bottom sashing strips, and two 2×7" sides sashing strips. Cut four 2" squares from the green fabric. All seams are sewn with right sides together unless otherwise specified. (All measurements include ½" seam allowances.)

With raw edges even, sew one sashing strip to the top of the stitchery and another to the bottom. Press the seams away from the stitchery. Sew a green square to both ends of the side sashing strips.

Sew one side sashing strip to the left side of the stitchery, matching the corner seams with the horizontal seam between the two pieces of sashing. Press the seams away from the stitchery. Attach the right sashing strip in the same manner. Press the seams toward the sashing strips.

Baste the fleece to the back stitched piece. Sew the front to the back with right sides together, leaving an opening to turn. Trim the seams and turn right side out. Slip-stitch the opening closed.

Baby Stocking

Supplies
14×18" piece of 14-count antique white
   wool Aida cloth
Cotton embroidery floss
10×14" piece of fusible fleece
½ yard of 45"-wide light blue-green
   print fabric

Continued

Hatching Christmas Cheer

Anchor		DMC	
9046	◇	321	Christmas red
923	▼	699	Dark Christmas green
227	☆	701	True Christmas green
305	✕	725	True topaz
295	⌃	726	Light topaz
293	⠄	727	Pale topaz
275	•	746	Off-white
309	◉	781	Dark topaz
307	▢	783	Christmas gold
133	♡	796	Royal blue
137	◆	798	Dark Delft blue
130	◎	809	True Delft blue
228	△	910	True emerald
205	○	912	Light emerald
340	♥	919	Red-copper
203	≡	954	Nile green
355	▦	975	Deep golden brown
1001	◪	976	Medium golden brown
1002	⌶	977	Light golden brown
887	✳	3045	Dark yellow-beige
886	⋈	3046	Medium yellow-beige
885	✚	3047	Light yellow-beige
292	⟍	3078	Lemon
382	■	3371	Black-brown
033	⊕	3706	Medium watermelon
031	‖	3708	Light watermelon
1098	★	3801	Deep watermelon
246	◗	3818	Deep emerald
1048	✦	3826	Dark golden brown
363	⌁	3827	Pale golden brown

BACKSTITCH

923	╱	699	Dark Christmas green – stems in border (2X)
382	╱	3371	Black-brown – all other stitches (1X)

Stitch count: 140 high x 79 wide

Finished design sizes:
14-count fabric – 10 x 5⅝ inches
16-count fabric – 8¾ x 5 inches
18-count fabric – 7¾ x 4⅜ inches

Hen stitch count: 69 high x 58 wide

Hen finished design sizes:
18-count fabric – 3¾ x 3¼ inches
16-count fabric – 4⅓ x 3⅝ inches
14-count fabric – 5 x 4⅛ inches

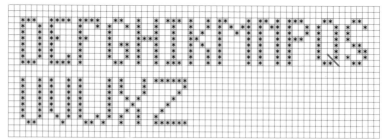

Baby Stocking Alphabet

⅛ yard of 45"-wide solid light
  blue-green fabric
1 yard of ¼"-diameter cording
Graph paper
Erasable fabric marker

Stitches

Chart the desired name on graph paper using the alphabet, *above,* and separating each letter with one square. Center and stitch the design on the fabric. Use three plies of floss to work the stitches unless otherwise specified. Press the stitchery from the back.

Assembly

Fuse the fleece to the back of the stitched piece following manufacturer's instructions. Use the erasable marker to draw the stocking outline as indicated by the dashed line on the chart. Cut out the stocking ½" beyond the marked line. Use the stocking as a pattern to cut a matching back and two lining pieces from the print fabric.

Cut a 1×6" hanging strip from the solid fabric. Also cut 2"-wide strips and piece to make a 30" piping strip from the solid fabric.

Center the cording lengthwise on the wrong side of the piping strip. Fold the fabric around the cording with the raw edges together. Use a zipper foot to sew through both layers close to the cording.

Press the long edges of the hanging strip under ¼", fold in half lengthwise, and topstitch. Fold the strip in half to form a loop. Tack the ends inside the top right side of the stocking.

Baste the cording around the sides and foot of the stocking front with the raw edges even. With right sides together, using the zipper foot, sew the stocking front to the back with a ½" seam allowance, leaving the top edge open. Trim the seam allowance to ¼".

Turn the stocking right side out and press. Sew the lining pieces together, right sides together, leaving an opening to turn; *do not* turn. Slip the stocking inside the lining. Stitch the stocking to the lining at the top edges; turn. Slip-stitch the opening closed. Tuck the lining into the stocking and press carefully.

Hoe! Hoe! Hoe! Stocking

Supplies

15×18" piece of 14-count country
  oatmeal Royal Classic fabric
Cotton embroidery floss
18×20" piece of fusible fleece
1 yard of 45"-wide tan-and-green print
  cotton fabric
1½ yards of ½"- diameter green
  sew-in cording
Graph paper
Erasable fabric marker

Stitches

Chart the desired name on graph paper using the alphabet on *page 61* and separating each letter with one square. Center and stitch the design from the stocking chart on the fabric. Use three plies of floss to work the stitches unless otherwise specified. Press the stitchery from the back.

Assembly

Fuse the fleece to the back of the stitched piece following the manufacturer's instructions. Use the erasable marker to draw the stocking outline as indicated by the dashed line on the chart. Cut out the stocking

½" beyond the marked line. Use the stocking as a pattern to cut a matching back and two lining pieces from the cotton fabric. Also cut a ¾×7" hanging strip from the cotton fabric.

Press the long edges of the hanging strip under ¼", fold in half lengthwise, and topstitch. Fold the strip in half to form a loop. Tack the ends inside the top right side of the stocking.

Baste the cording around the sides and foot of the stocking front with the raw edges even. With right sides together, use a zipper foot to sew the front to the back with a ½" seam allowance, leaving the top edge open. Trim the seam allowance to ¼".

Turn the stocking right side out and press. Sew the lining pieces together, right sides together, leaving an opening to turn; *do not* turn. Slip the stocking inside the lining. Stitch the stocking and lining together at the top edges; turn. Slip-stitch the opening closed. Tuck the lining into the stocking, and press carefully.

Holly Hat Band

Supplies

⅔ yard of 16-count 2"-wide celadon-
  and-white Aida-cloth banding
Cotton embroidery floss

Stitches

Center and stitch the holly motif from the stocking chart, *pages 60–61,* on the banding. Use two plies of floss to work the stitches unless otherwise specified. Repeat the motif as many times as needed to cover the length of the banding. Press the finished stitchery from the back. Position the banding around the hat as desired. Overlap the fabric at the back and slip-stitch the edges together.

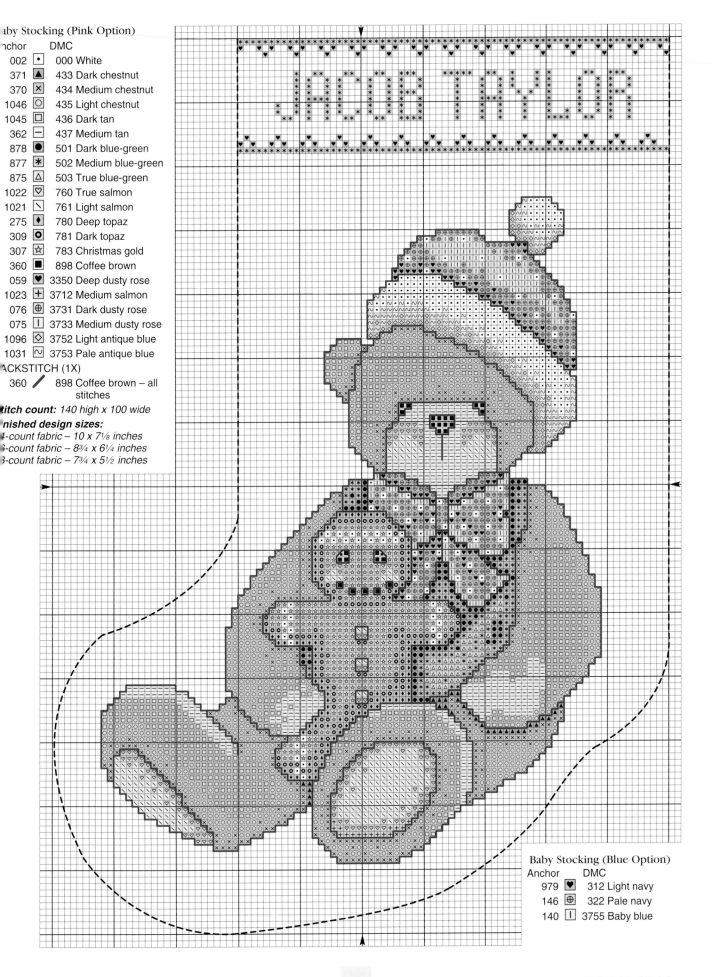

Baby Stocking (Pink Option)

Anchor		DMC	
002	·	000	White
371	▲	433	Dark chestnut
370	✕	434	Medium chestnut
1046	○	435	Light chestnut
1045	□	436	Dark tan
362	─	437	Medium tan
878	●	501	Dark blue-green
877	✳	502	Medium blue-green
875	△	503	True blue-green
1022	♡	760	True salmon
1021	＼	761	Light salmon
275	◆	780	Deep topaz
309	◓	781	Dark topaz
307	☆	783	Christmas gold
360	■	898	Coffee brown
059	♥	3350	Deep dusty rose
1023	＋	3712	Medium salmon
076	⊕	3731	Dark dusty rose
075	Ɪ	3733	Medium dusty rose
1096	◇	3752	Light antique blue
1031	∿	3753	Pale antique blue

BACKSTITCH (1X)

| 360 | ╱ | 898 | Coffee brown – all stitches |

Stitch count: 140 high x 100 wide

Finished design sizes:
14-count fabric – 10 x 7⅛ inches
16-count fabric – 8¾ x 6¼ inches
18-count fabric – 7¾ x 5½ inches

Baby Stocking (Blue Option)

Anchor		DMC	
979	♥	312	Light navy
146	⊕	322	Pale navy
140	Ɪ	3755	Baby blue

High-Spirited Holidays

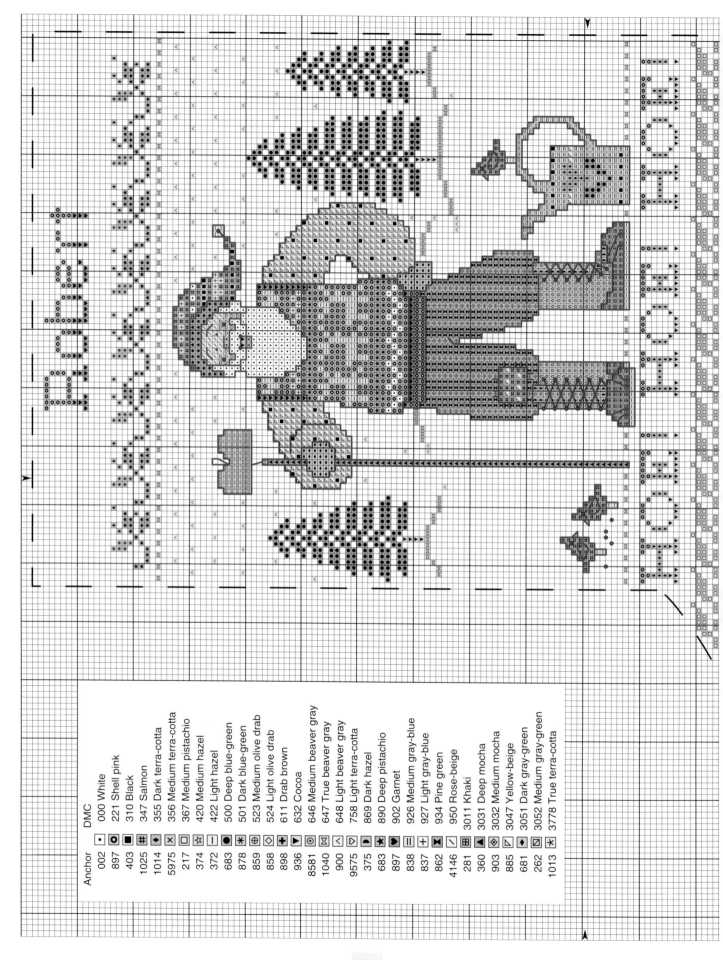

Anchor	DMC	
002	•	000 White
897	⊙	221 Shell pink
403	■	310 Black
1025	#	347 Salmon
1014	◆	355 Dark terra-cotta
5975	✕	356 Medium terra-cotta
217	▢	367 Medium pistachio
374	☆	420 Medium hazel
372	I	422 Light hazel
683	●	500 Deep blue-green
878	✳	501 Dark blue-green
859	⊕	523 Medium olive drab
858	◇	524 Light olive drab
898	✚	611 Drab brown
936	▶	632 Cocoa
8581	⊙	646 Medium beaver gray
1040	⊠	647 True beaver gray
900	<	648 Light beaver gray
9575	▷	758 Light terra-cotta
375	◣	869 Dark hazel
683	★	890 Deep pistachio
897	◗	902 Garnet
838	‖	926 Medium gray-blue
837	✛	927 Light gray-blue
862	◪	934 Pine green
4146	╱	950 Rose-beige
281	⊞	3011 Khaki
360	◀	3031 Deep mocha
903	◈	3032 Medium mocha
885	▽	3047 Yellow-beige
681	◆	3051 Dark gray-green
262	▨	3052 Medium gray-green
1013	✶	3778 True terra-cotta

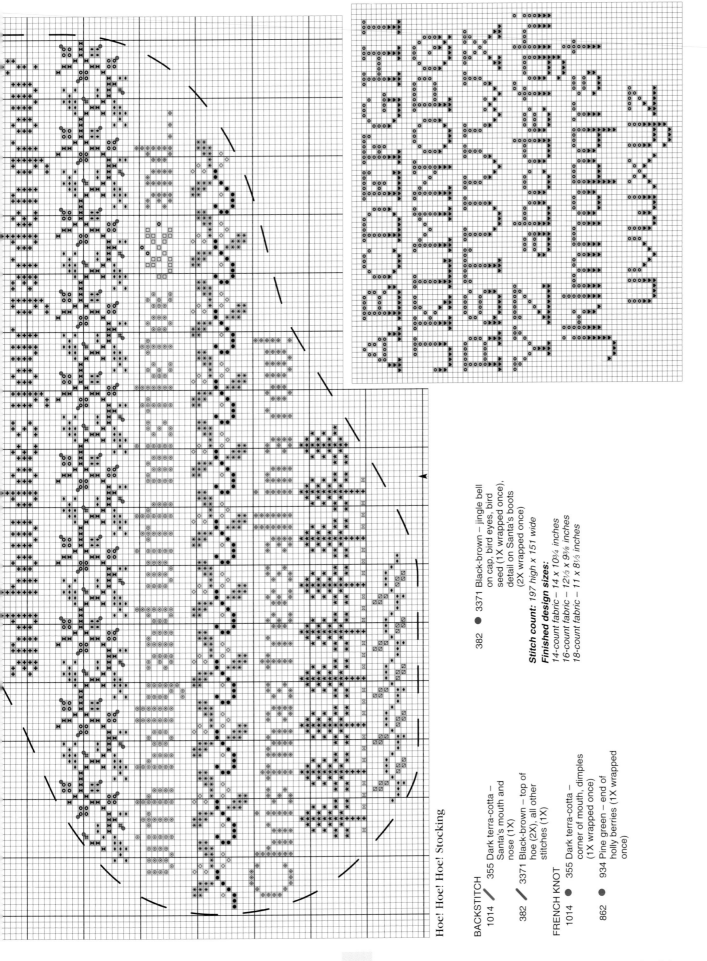

Hoe! Hoe! Hoe! Stocking

BACKSTITCH

1014 ╱ 355 Dark terra-cotta –
Santa's mouth and
nose (1X)

382 ╱ 3371 Black-brown – top of
hoe (2X), all other
stitches (1X)

FRENCH KNOT

1014 ● 355 Dark terra-cotta –
corner of mouth, dimples
(1X wrapped once)

862 ● 934 Pine green – end of
holly berries (1X wrapped
once)

382 ● 3371 Black-brown – jingle bell
on cap, bird eyes, bird
seed (1X wrapped once),
detail on Santa's boots
(2X wrapped once)

Stitch count: *197 high x 151 wide*

Finished design sizes:
14-count fabric – 14 x 10¾ inches
16-count fabric – 12⅓ x 9⅜ inches
18-count fabric – 11 x 8⅓ inches

High-Spirited Holidays

*At Christmas we
celebrate the birth
of Christ —*

*a gift of love that
remains the
overwhelming sentiment
of the season and a
guiding theme
for holiday stitching.*

Christmas Is Love

noel

Love came down
at Christmas...

STITCHED WITH LOVE BY GSB IN 2000

*I*f *soft-colored holiday decor appeals to you, stitch a sampler*
in shades of pastel pink and green. The piece speaks to the gentle love
of the infant born at Christmas.

*A*ngels, *a symbol of faith, are among the most beloved*
tree toppers. Stitch this one with metallic threads and beads to sparkle on the
highest branch or on a table top.

Designs: Love Came Down at Christmas, Gail Bussi; Faith Angel, Barbara Sestok

*D*isplay the loving warmth of Christmas on your furnishings with
comforting pillows adorned with holly and mistletoe. Stitch the whole chart on 14-count Aida
cloth to make an inviting square pillow, or work just the borders on banding
to adorn a bolster.

A nativity scene displayed for the holidays reminds us
of the true meaning of Christmas. This year stitch the holy family surrounded by
lifelike animals on 28-count Jobelan fabric.

Designs: The Heart of Christmas Is Love, Ursula Michael; Nativity, Barbara Sestok

*K*issing under the mistletoe, a custom rooted in
Scandinavian mythology, has become a playful expression of
seasonal affection. These friendly "Mistlesnow People," stitched on
14-count Aida cloth, continue the custom for another generation.

*C*reate a wreath of love for the holidays—five hearts
connected to form a star. Each heart is quick to stitch on 14-count white Aida cloth.
Or, stitch individual hearts on perforated paper for easy-finish ornaments.

Designs: Mistlesnow People, Robin Kingsley; Star of Hearts, Stephanie Novatski

Christmas Is Love

Love Came Down at Christmas Sampler

Supplies

*10×14" piece of 32-count antique ivory
   Belfast linen*
Cotton embroidery floss
#12 pearl cotton
Kreinik blending filament
Mill Hill seed beads and petite beads
Desired frame

Stitches

Center and stitch the design on the linen. Use two plies of floss to work the stitches over two threads of the fabric unless otherwise specified. Work the remaining stitches over the number of threads indicated on the chart and referring to the diagrams, *opposite*. For the Algerian eyelets, give each stitch a gentle tug to open a small hole. Attach the seed beads using one ply of floss. Press the stitchery facedown on a soft towel. Frame the piece as desired.

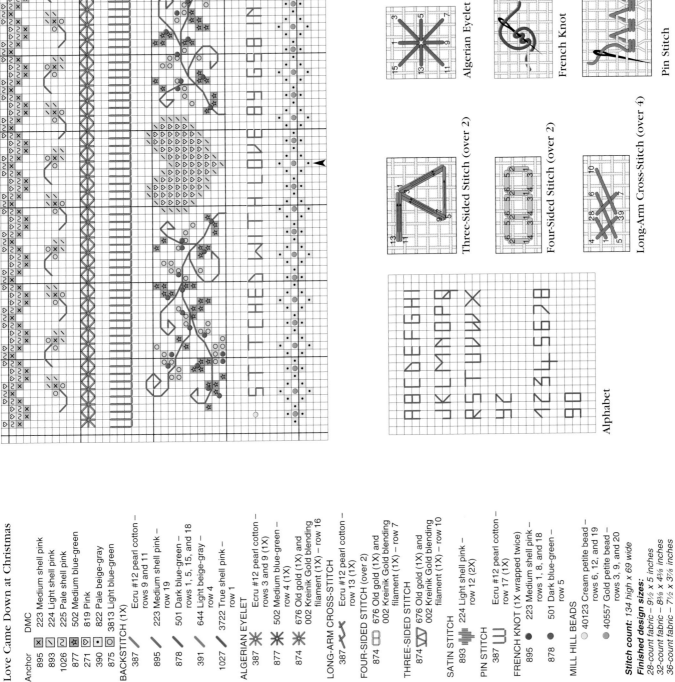

Love Came Down at Christmas

Anchor		DMC	
895	✕	223	Medium shell pink
893	◣	224	Light shell pink
1026	◢	225	Pale shell pink
877	✶	502	Medium blue-green
271	•	819	Pink
390	▷	822	Pale beige-gray
875	○	3813	Light blue-green

BACKSTITCH (1X)

387	Ecru #12 pearl cotton – rows 9 and 11
895	223 Medium shell pink – row 19
878	501 Dark blue-green – rows 1, 5, 15, and 18
391	644 Light beige-gray – row 4
1027	3722 True shell pink – row 1

ALGERIAN EYELET

387	✳	Ecru #12 pearl cotton – rows 3 and 9 (1X)
877	✱	502 Medium blue-green – row 4 (1X)
874	✸	676 Old gold (1X) and 002 Kreinik Gold blending filament (1X) – row 16

LONG-ARM CROSS-STITCH

387	⨯⨯	Ecru #12 pearl cotton – row 13 (1X)

FOUR-SIDED STITCH (over 2)

874	⊟	676 Old gold (1X) and 002 Kreinik Gold blending filament (1X) – row 7

THREE-SIDED STITCH

874	▽▽	676 Old gold (1X) and 002 Kreinik Gold blending filament (1X) – row 10

SATIN STITCH

893	▦	224 Light shell pink – row 12 (2X)

PIN STITCH

387	Ш	Ecru #12 pearl cotton – row 17 (1X)

FRENCH KNOT (1X wrapped twice)

895	●	223 Medium shell pink – rows 1, 8, and 18
878	●	501 Dark blue-green – row 5

MILL HILL BEADS

	○	40123 Cream petite bead – rows 6, 12, and 19
	●	40557 Gold petite bead – rows 3, 9, and 20

Stitch count: 134 high x 69 wide

Finished design sizes:
28-count fabric – 9½ x 5 inches
32-count fabric – 8⅜ x 4⅜ inches
36-count fabric – 7½ x 3⅞ inches

Algerian Eyelet (over 8)

Algerian Eyelet

French Knot

Pin Stitch

Three-Sided Stitch (over 2)

Four-Sided Stitch (over 2)

Long-Arm Cross-Stitch (over 4)

ABCDEFGHI
JKLMNOPQ
RSTUVWX
YZ
1234 5678
90

Alphabet

STITCHED WITH LOVE BY G58 IN 2000

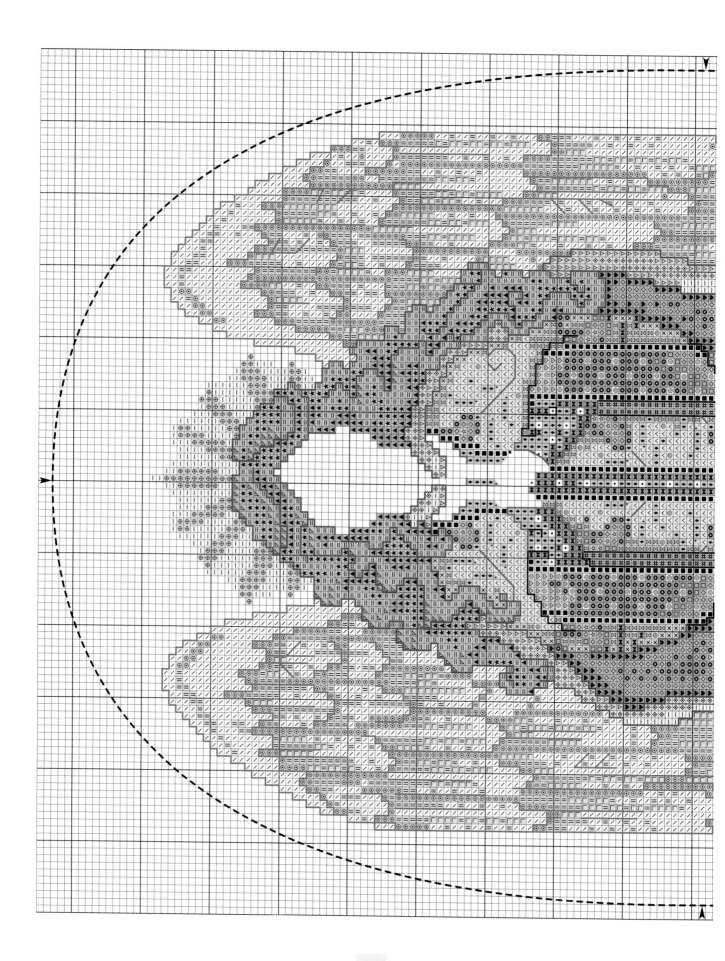

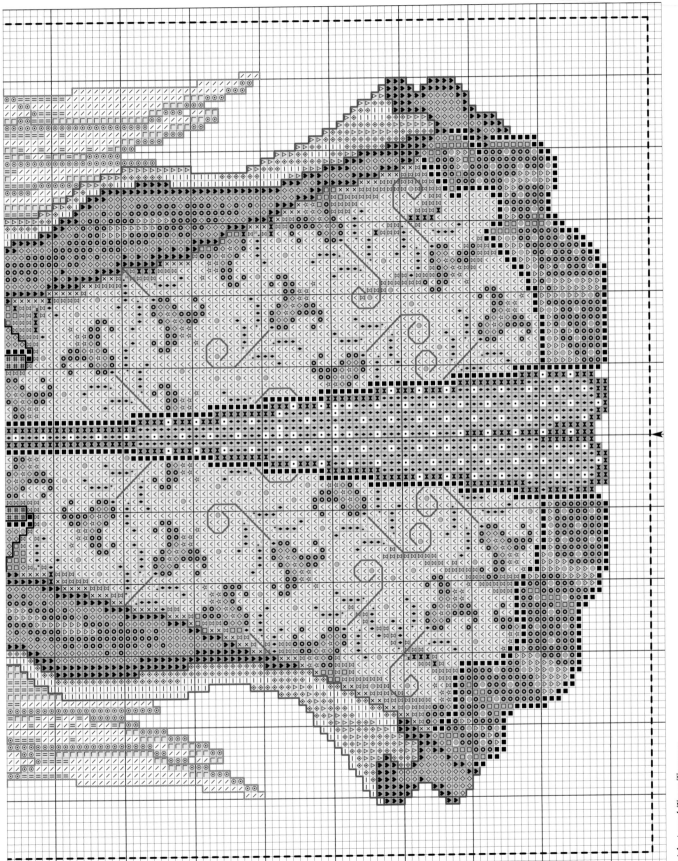

Faith Angel Tree Topper

Supplies

16×20" piece of 28-count light blue Jobelan fabric
Cotton embroidery floss
One additional skein each of white white (DMC B5200) and Nile green (DMC 913) floss
Kreinik blending filament
Kreinik #4 very fine braid
Mill Hill seed beads
Erasable fabric marker
½ yard of 45"-wide light blue sateen
16×20" piece of fleece
⅞ yard of ¼"-diameter metallic gold cord

Stitches

Center and stitch the design, *pages 72–74,* on the Jobelan fabric. Use three plies of floss to work the stitches over two threads of the fabric unless otherwise specified. For the face and hands, use one ply of floss to work the petite cross-stitches over one thread. Attach the seed beads using two plies of floss. Press the finished stitchery facedown on a soft towel.

Assembly

Use the marker to draw the topper outline as indicated by the dashed lines on the chart. Cut out the shape ½" beyond the marked outline. Use

Faith Angel Tree Topper
1 square = 1 thread

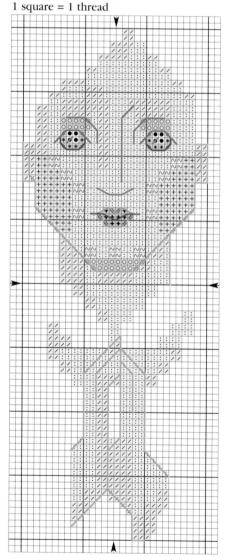

Anchor		DMC	
001	⊡	B5200	White white
403	●	310	Black
1025	◎	347	Deep salmon
233	⊞	451	Dark shell gray
1005	◻	498	Christmas red
923	◆	699	Christmas green
1021	+	761	Light salmon
275	★	780	Deep topaz
307	✼	783	Christmas gold
136	✳	799	Delft blue
358	▲	801	Coffee brown
043	◇	815	Medium garnet
376	◖	842	Beige-brown
897	♥	902	Deep garnet
227	✕	911	Medium emerald
204	△	913	Nile green
1012	⫶	948	Peach
4146	∕	950	Light rose-beige
039	✚	961	Rose-pink
1001	▤	976	Medium golden brown
035	♡	3705	Watermelon
1020	∿	3713	Pale salmon
	◼	005	Kreinik Black #4 very-fine braid
	⊕	028	Kreinik Citron #4 very-fine braid
	⊟	091	Kreinik Star yellow #4 very-fine braid

BLENDED NEEDLE

001	◺	B5200 White white (2X) and 032 Kreinik Pearl blending filament (1X)
232	◰	452 Medium shell gray (2X) and 192 Kreinik Pale pink blending filament (1X)
212 923	⊠	561 Seafoam (2X) and 699 Christmas green (1X)
305	◈	725 True topaz (2X) and 028 Kreinik Citron blending filament (1X)
307	▽	783 Christmas gold (2X) and 028 Kreinik Citron blending filament (1X)
168	◉	807 Peacock blue (2X) and 012 Kreinik Purple blending filament (1X)
168	⊞	807 Peacock blue (2X) and 032 Kreinik Pearl blending filament (1X)
227 205	⊠	911 Medium emerald (1X) and 912 Light emerald (2X)
1002	⊿	977 Light golden brown (2X) and 021 Kreinik Copper blending filament (1X)

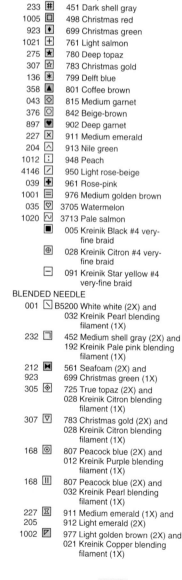

BACKSTITCH (1X)

001	∕	B5200 White white – eye highlights
136	∕	799 Delft blue – eyes
043	∕	815 Medium garnet – line between lips
039	∕	961 Rose-pink – mouth outline
883	∕	3064 Cocoa – eyelids
382	∕	3371 Black-brown – all other stitches
1008	∕	3773 Medium rose-beige – facial details, neck, and hands
	∕	005 Kreinik Black #4 very-fine braid – robe edging
	∕	009 Kreinik Emerald #4 very-fine braid – robe and flower stems on robe
	∕	025 Kreinik Grey #4 very-fine braid – wings

MILL HILL BEADS

●	02011 Victorian gold seed bead – robe detail
●	60161 Frosted crystal bead – robe detail

Angel stitch count: 169 high x 102 wide
Angel finished design sizes:
28-count fabric – 12 x 7¼ inches
32-count fabric – 10½ x 6⅓ inches
36-count fabric – 9⅜ x 5⅔ inches

Angel Face stitch count: 80 high x 30 wide
Angel Face finished design sizes:
(over one Thread)
28-count fabric – 2⅞ x 1 inches
32-count fabric – 2½ x ⅞ inches
36-count fabric – 2¼ x ¾ inches

the stitched fabric as a pattern to cut two interlinings from the fleece and one back and two lining pieces from the sateen fabric.

Baste one piece of fleece to the wrong side of the stitchery and the other to the satin back. Using the marker line as a guide, sew the front and back together, leaving the bottom open. Trim the seams and clip the curves; turn right side out. Sew the lining together in the same manner, leaving an opening in one side seam; *do not* turn. Set the lining aside.

Hand-stitch the cord to the seam line of the tree topper with the ends extending beyond the bottom edges. Slip the tree topper inside the lining. Sew the pieces together at the bottom edge with right sides together. Trim the seam and turn. Tuck the lining into the topper; press carefully. Slip-stitch the opening closed.

Heart of Christmas Square Pillow

Supplies
16" square of 14-count white Aida cloth
Cotton embroidery floss
One additional skein each of pistachio (DMC 368), old gold (DMC 729), and antique blue (DMC 932) floss
Kreinik #4 very fine braid
Mill Hill seed beads
½ yard of 45"-wide blue cotton fabric
1⅜ yard of ¼"-diameter cording
Polyester fiberfill

Stitches
Center and stitch the design, *pages 76–77,* on the Aida cloth. Use three

plies of floss or one strand of braid to work the stitches unless otherwise specified. Attach the seed beads using two plies of floss. Press the stitchery facedown on a soft towel.

Assembly
Centering the design, trim the stitchery to a 12" square. Use the stitchery as a pattern to cut a matching back from the blue fabric. Also from the blue fabric, cut 1⅞"-wide strips and join to make a 48"-long piping strip.

Center the cording lengthwise on the wrong side of the piping strip. Fold the fabric over the cording, with the long edges together. Using a zipper foot, sew close to the cording through all layers. Sew the piping around the perimeter of the pillow front with raw edges even.

Use ½" seams to sew the pillow front and back together with right sides facing and raw edges even, leaving an opening for turning. Trim the seams, clip the corners, and turn right side out. Press the pillow carefully. Stuff firmly with polyester fiberfill. Slip-stitch the opening closed.

Holly Banding Pillow

Supplies
2—16" lengths of 16-count white Aida cloth banding
Cotton embroidery floss
Kreinik #4 very fine braid
Mill Hill seed beads
½ yard of 45"-wide blue cotton fabric
1 yard of ¼"-diameter cording
White sewing thread
Polyester fiberfill

Stitches
Center and stitch the holly border from the chart, *pages 76–77,* on each length of banding, repeating the motif as needed. Use two plies of floss or one strand of braid to work the stitches unless otherwise specified. Attach the seed beads using two plies of floss. Place the stitchery facedown on a soft towel and carefully press from the back. Set the pieces aside.

Assembly
Cut a 15" square and two 5¾"-diameter end circles from the blue fabric. Also from the blue fabric, cut a 1⅞×30" piping strip.

To make the piping, center the cording lengthwise on the wrong side of the piping strip. Fold the fabric over the cording, with the long edges together. Using a zipper foot, sew close to the cording through all layers. Cut the cording in half.

With right sides together and raw edges even, baste one piece of piping to one edge of the square. Baste the remaining piping to the opposite edge of the square.

Pin one length of banding 1" from the piping at each end of the pillow. Use white sewing thread to topstitch the banding in place.

With right sides together, fold the fabric in half, and sew the unpiped edges together to form a tube, using a ½" seam and leaving an opening for turning; *do not* turn.

With right sides together, stitch the end panels to each end of the pillow next to the piping. Trim the seams and turn right side out. Stuff the pillow firmly with polyester fiberfill and slip-stitch the opening closed.

Nativity

Supplies
14×18" piece of 28-count denim blue Jobelan fabric
Cotton embroidery floss
Kreinik blending filament
Mill Hill seed beads
Desired frame

Continued

Stitches

Center and stitch the design, *pages 78–79,* on the Jobelan fabric. Use two plies of floss to work the stitches over two threads of the fabric unless otherwise specified. Attach the seed beads using two plies of floss. Press the stitchery facedown on a soft towel. Frame the piece as desired.

Heart of Christmas Is Love

Anchor		DMC	
013	⊞	349	Dark coral
010	◺	351	Light coral
214	⊞	368	Pistachio
1005	♥	498	Christmas red
891	▢	729	Old gold
379	✳	840	Medium beige-brown
378	◯	841	True beige-brown
376	❘	842	Light beige-brown
921	╱	932	Antique blue
246	●	986	Forest green
266	✕	3347	Medium yellow-green
862	⊟	3348	Light yellow-green
	⊡	191	Kreinik Pale yellow #4 very-fine braid

BACKSTITCH (1X)

043	╱	815	Garnet – ribbon outline
246	╱	986	Forest green – leaves, vines
	╱	191	Kreinik Pale yellow #4 very-fine braid – horizontal and vertical lines inside heart
	╱	221	Kreinik Antique gold #4 very-fine braid – heart outline and diagonal lines inside heart

BLENDED-NEEDLE BACKSTITCH

1005	╱	498	Christmas red (1X) and 221 Kreinik Antique gold #4 very-fine braid (1X) – lettering

MILL HILL BEADS

●	02013	Red red seed beads – berries in border, detail inside heart

Stitch count: 143 high x 143 wide
Finished design sizes:
14-count fabric – 10¼ x 10¼ inches
16-count fabric – 9 x 9 inches
18-count fabric – 8 x 8 inches

Mistlesnow People Pillow

Supplies

*14×16" piece of 14-count light blue Aida cloth
Cotton embroidery floss
Mill Hill seed beads
½ yard of 45"-wide pink cotton fabric
11½×11" piece of fusible fleece
1¼ yards of ½"-diameter cording
Polyester fiberfill*

Stitches

Center and stitch the design, *pages 80–81,* on the fabric. Use three plies of floss to work the stitches unless otherwise specified. Press the stitchery from the back.

Assembly

Centering the design, trim the stitchery to an 8"-high×8½"-wide rectangle. From the pink fabric, cut an 11½×11" back, two 2×8½" top and bottom sashing strips and two 2×11½" side sashing strips from the pink fabric. Also from the pink fabric, cut a 2×45"-long piping strip.

With raw edges even, sew one sashing strip to the top of the stitchery and another to the bottom using ¼" seams. Press the seams away from the stitchery. Sew one side sashing strip to each side of the stitchery. Press the seams away from the stitchery. Fuse the fleece to the back of the pieced pillow top following the manufacturer's instructions.

Center the cording lengthwise on the wrong side of the piping strip. Fold the fabric over the cording, with the long edges together. Using a zipper foot, sew close to the cording through all layers. Sew the piping around the perimeter of the pillow front with raw edges even.

Sew the pillow front and back together with right sides facing and raw edges even, leaving an opening for turning. Clip the corners, and turn right side out. Press the pillow carefully. Stuff the pillow firmly with polyester fiberfill and slip-stitch the opening closed.

Star of Hearts

Supplies

*5—7×8" pieces of 14-count white Aida cloth
Cotton embroidery floss
Kreinik blending filament
5—7×8" pieces of fusible fleece
¼ yard of 45"-wide white cotton fabric
Polyester fiberfill*

Stitches

Center and stitch the design, *page 81,* on the Aida cloth. Repeat to make a total of five hearts. Press the stitched pieces from the back.

Continued

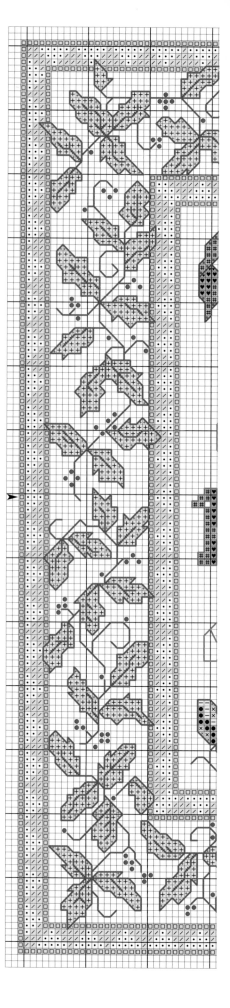

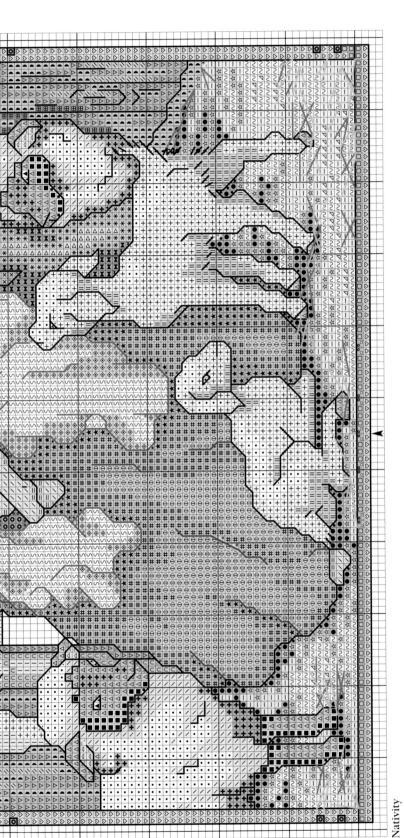

Nativity

Anchor	DMC	
926	⊞	378 841 True beige-brown
002	◉	360 898 Coffee brown
022	⊠	897 902 Garnet
148	◇	882 945 Dark ivory
401	△	1010 951 Medium ivory
914	*	903 3032 Medium mocha
407	∷	883 3064 Light cocoa
398	✳	266 3347 Medium yellow-green
374	▷	862 3348 Light yellow-green
372	◨	382 3371 Black-brown
371	◆	068 3687 True mauve
1045	□	076 3688 Medium mauve
1045	◻	1023 3712 Salmon
928	◄	169 3765 Deep peacock blue
855	▤	899 3782 Light mocha
936	●	236 3799 Charcoal
1040		**BLENDED NEEDLE**
900	◎	002 000 White (2X) and
874		032 Kreinik Pearl blending
885		filament (1X)
1016	◨	235 318 Light steel (2X) and
1039	⊞	001HL Kreinik Silver blending
379	⊠	filament (1X)

Ecru

926 ⊞ Ecru
002 ◉ 000 White
022 ⊠ 221 Shell pink
148 ◇ 311 Navy
401 △ 317 Pewter
914 * 407 Medium cocoa
407 ∷ 415 Pearl gray
398 ✳ 420 Medium hazel
374 ▷ 422 Light hazel
372 ◨ 433 Dark chestnut
371 ◆ 434 Medium chestnut
1045 □ 436 Tan
1045 ◻ 598 Turquoise
928 ◄ 612 Drab brown
855 ▤ 632 Deep cocoa
936 ● 647 True beaver gray
1040 648 Light beaver gray
900 ◎ 676 Light old gold
874 677 Pale old gold
885 778 Antique mauve
1016 806 Dark peacock blue
1039 840 Medium beige-brown

235	⊞	318 Light steel (2X) and
400		414 Dark steel (1X)
398		415 Pearl gray (2X) and
		032 Kreinik Pearl blending
		filament (1X)
168	⊕	807 Medium peacock blue (1X) and
167		3766 Light peacock blue (2X)
906	◼	829 Bronze (1X) and
375		869 Dark hazel (2X)
921	◈	932 Antique blue (2X) and
		032 Kreinik Pearl blending
		filament (1X)
903	⊞	3032 Medium mocha (1X) and
1050		3781 Dark mocha (2X)
292	◪	3078 Lemon (2X) and
		091 Kreinik Star yellow
		blending filament (1X)
268	⊠	3346 Hunter green (1X) and
266		3347 Medium yellow-green (2X)

HALF CROSS-STITCH (1X)
(stitch in direction of symbol)

148 ╱ 311 Navy – background

BACKSTITCH

022 ╱ 221 Shell pink – mouths (2X) and
148 ╱ 311 Navy – Mary's gown detail (1X)
371 ╱ 433 Dark chestnut – Baby's hair (1X)
1045 ╱ 436 Tan – cuff and front of Mary's robe (1X)
897 ╱ 902 Garnet – Mary's robe border (1X)
382 ╱ 3371 Black-brown – all other stitches (1X)
╱ 010HL Kreinik Steel gray blending filament – Baby's blanket (1X)

STRAIGHT STITCH

371 ╱ 433 Dark chestnut – Joseph's eyebrows (3X), hay (2X)
307 ╱ 783 Christmas gold – dove beaks (2X)
360 ╱ 898 Coffee brown – Mary's eyebrows (2X)
382 ╱ 3371 Black-brown – facial features, Baby's legs, and sheep (1X)

BLENDED-NEEDLE STRAIGHT STITCH

885 ╱ 677 Pale old gold (1X) and
307 783 Christmas gold (1X) – hay

SATIN STITCH (2X)

1023 ╱ 3712 Salmon – mouths

SMYRNA CROSS-STITCH (1X)

✳ 094 Kreinik Star blue #8 fine braid – stars

FRENCH KNOT (2X wrapped once)

382 ● 3371 Black-brown – Mary, Baby's, and dove eyes

MILL HILL BEADS

○ 00557 Gold seed beads – Baby's halo

Stitch count: 153 high x 108 wide

Finished design sizes:
28-count fabric – 11 x 7¾ inches
32-count fabric – 9½ x 6¾ inches
36-count fabric – 8½ x 6 inches

Christmas Is Love

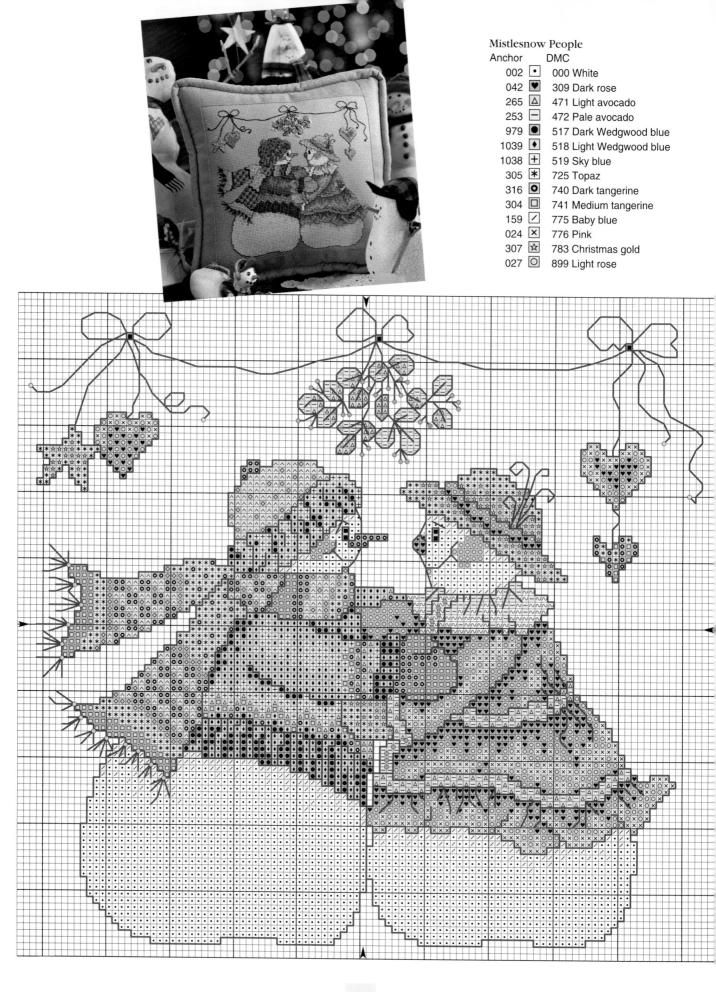

Mistlesnow People

Anchor		DMC	
002	·	000	White
042	♥	309	Dark rose
265	△	471	Light avocado
253	−	472	Pale avocado
979	●	517	Dark Wedgwood blue
1039	♦	518	Light Wedgwood blue
1038	+	519	Sky blue
305	✳	725	Topaz
316	◉	740	Dark tangerine
304	☐	741	Medium tangerine
159	╱	775	Baby blue
024	✕	776	Pink
307	☆	783	Christmas gold
027	○	899	Light rose

228	◈	910 True emerald
205	⌃	912 Light emerald
381	◼	938 Coffee brown
386	∼	3823 Yellow

BACKSTITCH

381 / 938 Coffee brown – swag (2X),
all other stitches (1X)

FRENCH KNOT

381 ● 938 Coffee brown – swag
and scarf fringe (2X
wrapped twice)

MILL HILL BEADS

● 60161 Frosted crystal beads –
buttons, mistletoe

Stitch count: *96 high x 105 wide*

Finished design sizes:
14-count fabric – 6⅞ x 7½ inches
16-count fabric – 6 x 6½ inches
18-count fabric – 5⅓ x 5⅞ inches

Assembly

For each heart, fuse fleece to the back of the stitchery following the manufacturer's instructions. Use the erasable marker to draw an outline ⅜" beyond the outermost stitching. Cut out on the marked line. Use the stitched piece as a pattern to cut a matching back from the white fabric.

Sew the front to the back with right sides together using ¼" seams and leaving an opening for turning. Clip to, but not through, the seam at the top center. Trim the seam at the bottom point. Turn right side out. Stuff firmly with polyester fiberfill and slip-stitch the opening closed. Repeat with the remaining shapes. Hand-sew the hearts together at the positions indicated by the X's on the chart.

Heart Ornaments

Supplies

For each ornament
5½" square of 14-count white
perforated paper
Cotton embroidery floss
Kreinik blending filament
5½" square each of white and red felt
½ yard of 1"-wide red organdy ribbon
Crafts glue

Stitches

Center and stitch the heart design on the perforated paper. Cut out the heart shape one square beyond the stitched area.

Assembly

Center and glue the stitched paper atop the white felt. Trim the felt ⅛" beyond the edges of the paper. Center and glue the ornament atop the red felt; cut out ⅛" beyond the white felt.

Tie the ribbon in a bow. Tack the bow to the top center of the heart. Trim the ribbon ends.

Star of Hearts

Anchor		DMC
BLENDED NEEDLE		
9046	♡	321 Christmas red (2X) and 002 Kreinik Gold blending filament (1X)
874	▫	676 Light old gold (2X) and 002HL Kreinik Gold Hi Lustre blending filament (1X)
891	⊞	729 Medium old gold (2X) and 003 Kreinik Red blending filament (1X)

Stitch count: *55 high x 50 wide*

Finished design sizes:
14-count fabric – 3⅞ x 3½ inches
16-count fabric – 3⅜ x 3⅛ inches
18-count fabric – 3 x 2¾ inches

To *stitch up a country-style Christmas*, combine homespun simplicity with a touch of nature.

~

Festive Folk Art

S*pice up a country tree with simple folk art motifs in rich shades*

of red and green, stitched on 32-count linen. They're so easy

to finish, you'll want to stitch some extras for gifts.

H*ere's a Christmas tree for any room*

of the house. Attach the checkerboard tree, stitched on 28-count linen and adorned with stars, to a simple

cotton flannel pillow with running stitches, and finish with yellow star buttons.

Designs: Folk Art Ornaments, Heart in Hand Needlework; O' Christmas Tree, Kathy Moenkhaus

If you love folk art style,

stitch some heart-shape ornaments on 14-count country Aida cloth.

They're sure to draw attention to a country-style tree, or to a basket of wood shavings.

Greet the holidays with a special wish

stitched on 14-count Aida cloth and finished with a twig frame.

Designs: Sampler Heart Ornaments, Robin Clark; Have a Merry Little Christmas, Lizzie Kate

Festive Folk Art

Welcome friends and family home

for the holidays with a familiar song title that's easy to stitch on 18-count linen.

Then, give the piece a rustic touch with a barn-board frame.

Design: I'll Be Home for Christmas, Bent Creek

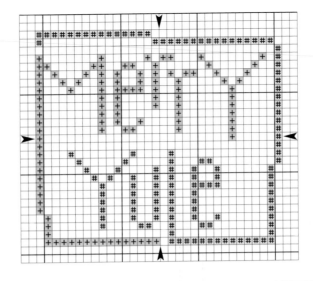

*F*olk Art Ornaments

Supplies

For each ornament
6" square of 32-count sandstone linen
Cotton embroidery floss
Fusible fleece
6" square of Ultrasuede or felt
Sewing thread

Stitches

Center and stitch the design on the linen. Use two plies of floss to work the stitches over two threads of fabric unless otherwise specified. Press the stitchery from the back.

Assembly

Measure the height and width of the stitched area and cut a square or rectangle of fleece ½" larger in each direction. Center and fuse the fleece to the back of the stitchery following the manufacturer's instructions. Trim the excess fabric ⅝" beyond the stitched area. Position the stitchery atop the suede fabric. Machine topstitch ¼" beyond the stitching. To make the fringe, remove the threads between the topstitching and the linen edge.

For the twisted hanger, cut one 2-yard six-ply length of dark blue-green (DMC 501) and two 2-yard six-ply lengths of shell pink (DMC 221) floss. Combine the plies into a single strand. Secure one end of the joined strands and twist until tightly wound. Holding the ends, fold the strand in half as the two halves twist around each other. Knot both ends to secure them. Tie a knot in the center of the cord. Tack the cord ends to the ornament back.

Folk Art Ornaments

Anchor		DMC
897	+	221 Shell pink
374	○	420 Hazel
683	◆	500 Deep blue-green
878	#	501 Dark blue-green
360	●	839 Beige-brown

Merry Yule stitch count:
 27 high x 32 wide

Merry Yule finished design sizes:
32-count fabric – 1⅝ x 2 inches
28-count fabric – 2 x 2¼ inches
36-count fabric – 1½ x 1¾ inches

Primitive Star stitch count:
 27 high x 27 wide

Primitive Star finished design sizes:
32-count fabric – 1⅝ x 1⅝ inches
28-count fabric – 2 x 2 inches
36-count fabric – 1½ x 1½ inches

Primitive Tree stitch count:
 46 high x 27 wide

Primitive Tree finished design sizes:
32-count fabric – 2⅞ x 1⅝ inches
28-count fabric – 3¼ x 2 inches
36-count fabric – 2½ x 1½ inches

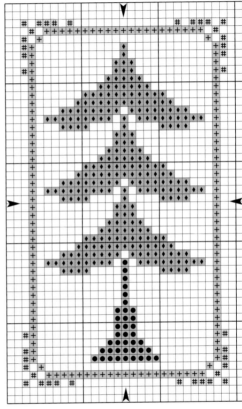

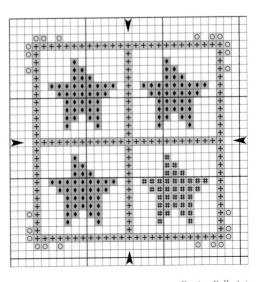

O' Christmas Tree

The chart legend reads:

Anchor		DMC
897	♥	221 Shell pink
945	−	834 Bronze
905	●	3021 Brown-gray
681	◆	3051 Dark gray-green
262	✕	3052 Medium gray-green

Stitch count: 118 high x 98 wide
Finished design sizes:
28-count fabric – 8⅜ x 7 inches
32-count fabric – 7⅜ x 6⅛ inches
36-count fabric – 6½ x 5⅜ inches

O' Christmas Tree Pillow

The finished pillow is 14×15".

Supplies

20" square of 28-count natural linen
Cotton embroidery floss
⅔ yard of 45"-wide rust plaid fabric
10½×12" piece of lightweight fusible interfacing
Polyester fiberfill
4—1"-diameter yellow star buttons

Stitches

Center and stitch the chart on the linen. Use two plies of floss to work the cross-stitches over two threads of the fabric unless otherwise specified. Press the stitchery from the back.

Assembly

Centering the design, trim the stitched piece to a 10½×12" rectangle. Center and fuse the interfacing to the back following the manufacturer's instructions. Press the edges of the stitchery under ½". Set the stitchery aside.

Cut two 15×16" rectangles from the plaid fabric. (All measurements include ½" seam allowances.) Center the wrong side of the stitchery on the right side of the one plaid rectangle. Use four plies of shell pink floss (DMC 221) to work running stitches around the edges of the stitched linen ¼" from the folded edges.

Sew the pillow front and back together with right sides together and raw edges even leaving an opening for turning. Trim the seams, clip the corners, and turn right side out; press carefully. Stuff the pillow firmly with polyester fiberfill, and slip-stitch the opening closed. Sew a star button to each corner of the pillow.

Sampler Heart Ornaments

Supplies

For each ornament
8" square of 14-count Fiddler's Lite, Fiddler's green, Fiddler's rose, or Fiddler's blue Aida cloth
Cotton embroidery floss
Erasable fabric marker
Tracing paper
5×6" piece of self-stick mounting board with foam
4×5½" piece of green felt
⅜ yard of 45"-wide green-and-red plaid fabric
14½" length of ¼"-diameter cording
Crafts glue

Stitches

Center and stitch the desired heart chart, *pages 92–93*, on the desired fabric. Use three plies of floss to work the stitches unless otherwise specified. Press the stitchery from the back.

Assembly

Use the erasable marker to draw the ornament outline onto the back of the Aida cloth as indicated by the dashed lines on the chart; *do not* cut out. Place the tracing paper over the fabric and trace the ornament outline. Cut out the paper pattern. Use the paper pattern to cut matching shapes from the mounting board and the felt.

Peel the protective paper from the mounting board. Match the foam side to the outline on the back of the stitchery; press to stick. Trim the fabric ½" beyond the edges. Fold the excess fabric to the back; glue.

Cut a 1½×18" bias piping strip and a 1"×6" bias hanging strip from the plaid fabric.

Center the cording lengthwise on the wrong side of the piping strip. Fold the fabric around the cording with the raw edges together. Use a zipper foot to sew through both layers close to the cording.

Position and glue the covered cord around the edge of the ornament, overlapping the ends at the bottom center. Trim the excess cord; glue the ends to the back. For the hanger, press the long edges of the hanging strip under ¼", fold in half lengthwise, and topstitch. Fold the strip in half to form a loop. Glue the ends to the top center back of the ornament. Glue the felt to the back of the ornament.

Have a Merry Little Christmas

Supplies

13×18" piece of 14-count navy Aida cloth
Sampler Threads overdyed floss
4½×10" mounting board
4½×10" piece of fleece
4½×10" piece navy construction paper
2—½"-diameter 12½"-long straight twigs
2—½"-diameter 6¾"-long straight twigs
Spray adhesive
Crafts and wood glue
Crafts knife
Drill and pilot screw
8 small nails

Continued

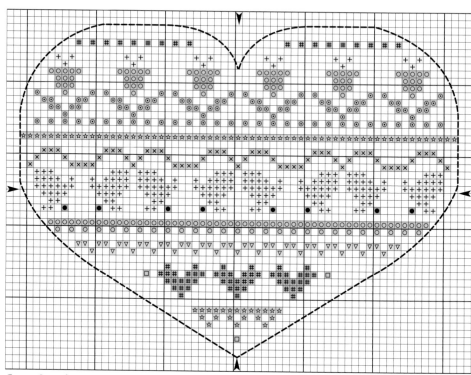

Sampler Hearts Ornaments

Anchor		DMC
897	▦	221 Shell pink
218	☐	319 Pistachio
1025	○	347 Salmon
1014	✕	355 Terra-cotta
683	▲	500 Deep blue-green
878	◉	501 Dark blue-green
889	◆	610 Deep drab brown
855	☆	612 Medium drab brown
853	⎮	613 Light drab brown
874	+	676 Old gold
072	♥	902 Garnet
837	=	927 Gray-blue
862	★	934 Pine green
905	●	3021 Deep brown-gray
040	◇	3023 Light brown-gray
262	▽	3052 Gray-green

Stitch count: *46 high x 63 wide*
Finished design sizes:
14-count fabric – 3¼ x 4½ inches
16-count fabric – 2⅞ x 4 inches
18-count fabric – 2½ x 3½ inches

Tan Sampler Heart

Green Sampler Heart

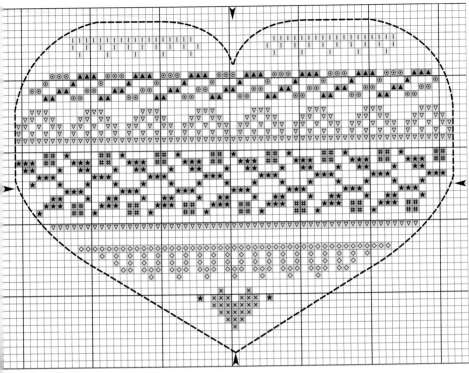

Rose Sampler Heart

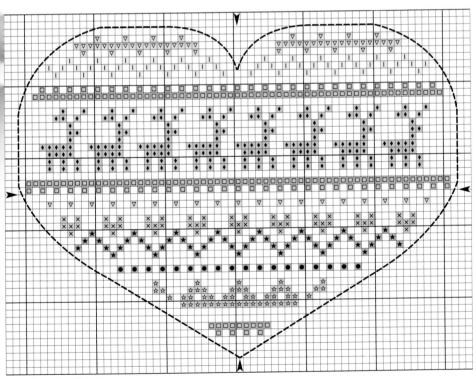

Blue Sampler Heart

Stitches

Center and stitch the design, *page 94,* on the fabric. Use two plies of floss to work the stitches. When using overdyed floss, complete each individual stitch before proceeding to the next one. Press from the back.

Assembly

Spray the mounting board lightly with adhesive and position the fleece on top. Center the wrong side of the stitchery over the fleece-covered board. Tape or glue the edges to the back. Set the piece aside.

For the frame, measure and mark ½" and again ¾" from one end of one 12½" twig. Use the crafts knife to cut a ⅛"-deep notch between the marks. Repeat for the other end of the twig. Cut notches in the remaining twigs in the same manner.

Lay the 12½" twigs parallel to each other with notches facing up. Position the 6¾" twigs across the long twigs, matching notches. Check the fit of the stitchery. It should fit snugly within the frame. Adjust the frame by cutting larger notches if necessary. Remove the stitchery and use wood glue to join the twigs at the corner intersections. Let the glue dry.

Drill small pilot holes from front to back through twigs at the corner intersections. Also drill though the side at the center of each twig. Insert a small nail into each corner; bend the point of the nail to the side.

Position the stitchery in the frame. Insert a small nail through the pilot holes in the sides of the frame then into the mounting board to secure the piece in the frame. Use crafts glue to adhere the construction paper to the back of the stitched piece.

For the hanger, thread a needle with a 10" six-ply length of navy floss and knot the end. Insert the needle into the top right corner of the stitchery back; repeat for the other side of the stitchery. Tie the ends of the floss in a knot at the top center.

Festive Folk Art

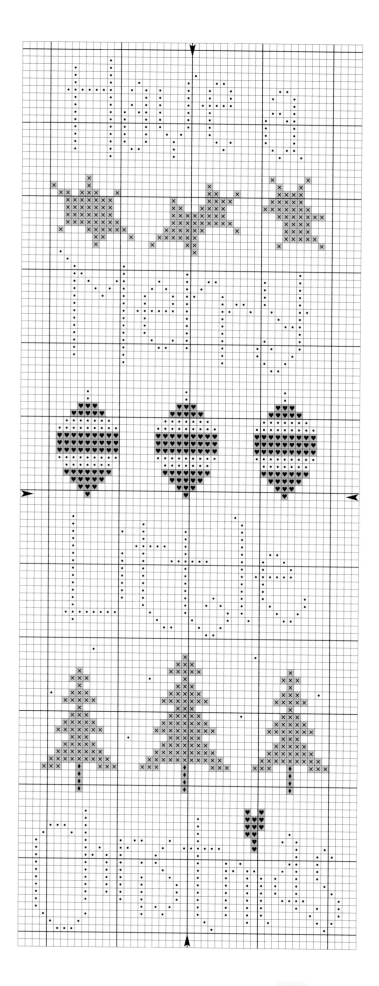

Have a Merry Little Christmas

Anchor	DMC	Gentle Arts Sampler Threads	
212 ☒	561	0120	Pine
1006 ♥	304	0330	Cherry wine
905 ◆	3021	1110	Sable
926 •	712	1140	Oatmeal

Stitch count: 119 high x 44 wide
Finished design sizes:
14-count fabric – 8½ x 3⅛ inches
16-count fabric – 7½ x 2¾ inches
18-count fabric – 6⅔ x 2½ inches

I'll Be Home for Christmas

Supplies
14×16″ piece of 18-count
    rosemary linen
Cotton embroidery floss
Desired frame

Stitches
Center and stitch the design on the linen. Use four plies of floss to work the stitches over two threads of the fabric unless otherwise specified. Press the stitched piece from the back. Frame the piece as desired.

Colonial Knot

Smyrna Cross-Stitch (over 4)

I'll Be Home for Christmas

Anchor		DMC (4X)	
890	[O]	680	Old gold
380	◆	838	Deep beige-brown
379	☆	840	Medium beige-brown
375	#	869	Hazel
897	♥	902	Garnet
862	▲	934	Deep pine green
269	✕	936	Medium pine green
391	·	3033	Mocha

BACKSTITCH
380	╱	838 Deep beige-brown – windows (2X)

SMYRNA CROSS-STITCH
002	✳	000 White – stars in background (4X)

SATIN STITCH
391	⦀	3033 Mocha – blocks on house (4X)

COLONIAL KNOT
862	●	934 Deep pine green – wreath (4X)

Stitch count: *91 high x 74 wide*

Finished design sizes:
18-count fabric – 10⅛ x 8¼ inches
25-count fabric – 7¼ x 6 inches
32-count fabric – 5⅝ x 4⅝ inches

*D*eck your
holiday halls
*with a sampling of
traditional stitches
and motifs.*

Simply Samplers

*T*reat yourself to the luxury of stitching with silk thread

to create a lacy poinsettia sampler. Though relatively easy to stitch on 28-count linen,

when surrounded by an ornate frame, this piece recalls ornate Victorian samplers.

*S*hare the joy of Christmas with a simply stitched holiday sampler.

Worked on 18-count linen and embellished with a sterling silver charm,

it's an excellent choice for the beginning stitcher.

Designs: Poinsettia Sampler, Kandace Thomas; Christmas Joy, Shepherd's Bush

*F*or a quick gift, stitch a
holiday greeting on linen and finish it as a needle
roll that doubles as a tree ornament. Repeat the
motifs from the Happy Holidays chart on banding
to make an ordinary candle stand out. Rearrange
the Merry Christmas chart to make a
special yuletide greeting.

Design: Holiday Greetings, Phyllis Dobbs

*L*acy and light, this ornament sampler

pillow features a rayon floss border of snowflakes and old-time ornaments

worked in hand-dyed threads on 28-count linen. It offers a multitude of options for individual tree trims.

For variety, the ornaments above were stitched on

14-count Aida with variegated and white cotton floss.

Design: Winter Bulbs Sampler, Margaret Lee Rigiel

*T*he motifs of this sampler reflect the sentimental verse

that starts it off. It's stitched on 28-count linen and finished with a simple

brass hanger and gold tassel.

Design: Christmas in the Air, Linda Reeves

Poinsettia Sampler

Supplies
16" square of 28-count laurel linen
Kreinik Soie d'Alger silk floss
Kreinik blending filament
Desired frame

Stitches
Center and stitch the design on the linen fabric. Use three plies of floss to work the stitches over two threads of the fabric unless otherwise specified. Press the finished stitchery facedown on a soft towel. Frame as desired.

Christmas Joy Sampler

Supplies
14×18" piece of 18-count lambswool linen
Sampler Threads overdyed floss
Shepherd's Bush 7/16"-tall folk heart charm

Stitches
Center and stitch the design, *page 106,* on the fabric. Use four plies of floss to work the stitches over two threads of the fabric unless otherwise specified. When working with overdyed floss, complete each individual stitch before proceeding to the next one. Attach the heart charm using one ply of floss. Press the stitchery facedown on a soft towel. Frame the piece as desired.

Holiday Greetings Needle Rolls

Supplies
2—10" squares of 28-count star sapphire linen
Cotton embroidery floss
Needle Necessities overdyed #8 pearl cotton
Kreinik #4 very fine braid
Mill Hill seed beads
4—15" lengths of 1/8"-wide burgundy satin ribbon
Polyester fiberfill

Stitches
Center and stitch one design, *page 107,* on each square of linen. Use two plies of floss to work the stitches over two threads unless otherwise specified. When using overdyed thread,

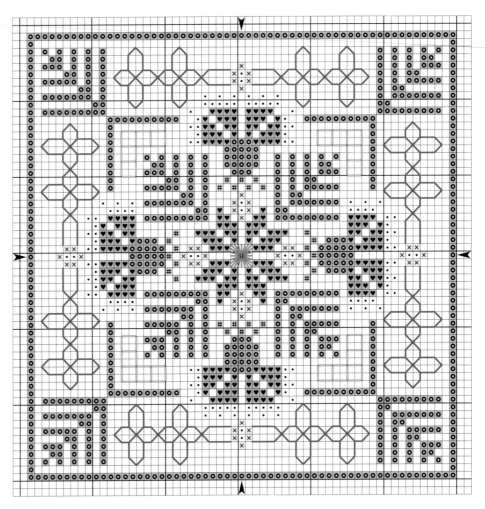

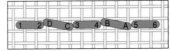

Double Running Stitch

complete each individual stitch before proceeding to the next one. Attach the seed beads using two plies of floss. Press facedown on a soft towel.

Assembly
Trim the fabric ½" beyond the stitching on the sides, and 2" beyond at the the top and bottom. Fold under the top edge under ¼" twice; topstitch. Repeat at the bottom.

With right sides together and raw edges even, sew the unhemmed edges together with a ½" seam to make a tube. Turn the tube right side out. Thread a needle with a doubled length of thread. Run a gathering thread 1" from the top edge of the fabric. Pull tightly to close the end; secure the thread. Run a gathering thread at the bottom end, but *do not* secure. Stuff

Continued

Poinsettia Sampler

Kreinik

Soie d'Alger	Anchor		DMC
Creme	986	•	Ecru
1844	862	◉	520 Deep olive drab
1843	860	⌗	522 Dark olive drab
2925	1005	♥	816 Garnet
BLENDED NEEDLE			
2532	874	✕	676 Old gold (2X) and Kreinik 002 Gold blending filament (1X)
FOUR-SIDED STITCH (1X)			
Creme	387	▢	Ecru
DOUBLE-RUNNING STITCH (1X)			
1843	860	╱	522 Dark olive drab
ALGERIAN EYELET (1X)			
1844	862	✳	520 Deep olive drab

Stitch count: 59 high x 59 wide

Finished design sizes:
28-count fabric – 4¼ x 4¼ inches
32-count fabric – 3⅝ x 3⅝ inches
25-count fabric – 4¾ x 4¾ inches

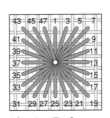

Algerian Eyelet

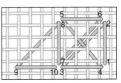

Four Sided Stitch

Christmas Joy

Anchor		DMC	Sampler Threads	
683	◆	500	0140	Blue spruce
119	●	333	0230	Blueberry
043	♥	815	0360	Cranberry
1024	✕	3328	0380	Raspberry parfait
118	○	340	0850	Hyacinth
212	+	561	0930	Deep sea
360	■	839	1110	Sable
926	−	Ecru	1140	Oatmeal
372	╱	422	1150	Flax
4146	•	950		Rose-beige

BACKSTITCH (2X)

683	╱	500	0140	Blue spruce – holly leaves
043	╱	815	0360	Cranberry – hat and pants
212	╱	561	0930	Deep sea – hat tassel
360	╱	839	1110	Sable – holly vine and stems, Santa's staff

ATTACHMENTS

✕   Shepherd's Bush folk heart charm – Santa's staff

Stitch count: 65 high x 28 wide
Finished design sizes:
18-count fabric – 7¼ x 3⅛ inches
32-count fabric – 4 x 1¾ inches
28-count fabric – 4⅝ x 2 inches

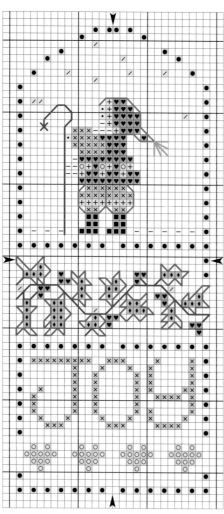

Christmas Joy

the tube firmly with polyester fiberfill. Pull the thread at the bottom end tightly and secure. Tie a length of ribbon around the gathers. Tie the ribbon in a bow; trim the ribbon ends.

Candle Banding

Supplies
Pillar candle
2⅞"-wide 27-count antique white/ red/green woven hearts linen banding 2" longer than the candle circumference
Wildflowers overdyed thread
Wildflowers solid colored threads
Kreinik #4 very-fine braid
Mill Hill seed beads

Stitches
Begin stitching one end of the chart at one end of the banding. Use one strand of thread to work the stitches over two threads of fabric unless otherwise specified. When using

overdyed thread, complete each individual stitch before proceeding to the next one. Attach the seed beads using one strand of thread.

Repeat the motifs as needed to circle the candle. Press the finished stitchery facedown on a soft towel. Position the banding around the candle as desired. Overlap the fabric at the back and slip-stitch the edges together.

Merry Christmas Card

Supplies
7×8" piece of 26-count ivory linen
Cotton embroidery floss
Waterlilies overdyed silk floss
Mill Hill seed beads
4½×6" piece of fusible interfacing
Purchased 5×7" tri-fold holly embossed Christmas green card with a 3½×5" opening

Stitches
Measure 1" from the top and 1½" from the side of the linen. Begin stitching the top row of Part 1 of the chart. Work the stitches using the number of plies indicated in the key. Attach the seed beads using two plies of floss. When Part 1 is complete, stitch Part 2. Press the finished stitchery facedown on a soft towel.

Assembly
Centering the design, fuse the interfacing to the wrong side of the stitchery. Trim the excess fabric beyond the interfacing edges. Tape the stitchery to the inside of the card.

Winter Bulbs Pillow

Supplies
20" square of 28-count dark teal green Cashel linen fabric
Cotton embroidery floss
White rayon floss
Weeks Dyeworks overdyed floss
Kreinik #8 braid
Mill Hill seed beads
13" square of fusible fleece
⅛ yard of 45"-wide burgundy fabric
½ yard of 45"-wide purple fabric
1⅓ yards each of ¼"-diameter and ½"-diameter cording
Polyester fiberfill

Continued

Merry Christmas Card

Anchor		DMC	
239	−	702	Christmas green (3X)
	✕	002	Kreinik Gold #4 very-fine braid (1X)

BACKSTITCH (3X)

042	╱	309	Rose – lettering

SATIN STITCH (4X)

||||| 025 Waterlilies Holiday overdyed thread

DIAMOND EYELET (8 over 4)

239	✳	702	Christmas green (3X)

RHODES-STITCH HEART (4X)

✻ 025 Waterlilies Holiday overdyed thread

MILL HILL BEADS

◎ 02011 Victorian gold seed bead

Stitch count: 61 high x 37 wide
Finished design sizes:
26-count fabric – 4⅝ x 2⅞ inches
28-count fabric – 4⅓ x 2⅝ inches
32-count fabric – 3⅞ x 2⅓ inches

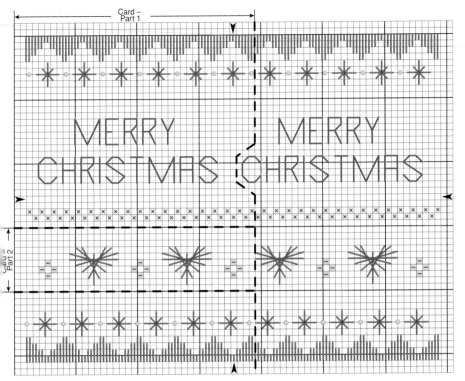

Holiday Greeting—Merry Christmas

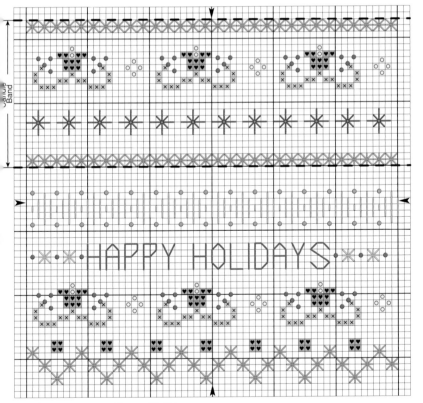

Holiday Greetings—Happy Holidays

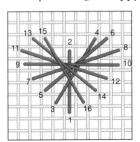

Rhodes-Stitch Heart

Diamond Eyelet

Smyrna Cross-Stitch Over 4

Merry Christmas Needle Roll

Anchor		DMC	
212	⊟	561	Seafoam
	⊠	002	Kreinik Gold #4 very-fine braid

BACKSTITCH (3X)

045	╱	814	Garnet – lettering

SATIN STITCH (1X)

	‖‖‖	851	Needle Necessities Christmas Eve #8 overdyed pearl cotton

DIAMOND EYELET (8 over 4)

212	✳	561	Seafoam (3X)

RHODES-STITCH HEART (1X)

	✳	851	Needle Necessities Christmas Eve #8 overdyed pearl cotton

MILL HILL BEADS

	◦	02011	Victorian gold seed bead

Stitch count: 51 high x 67 wide

Finished design sizes:
28-count fabric – 3⅝ x 4¾ inches
32-count fabric – 3⅛ x 4⅛ inches
36-count fabric – 2⅞ x 3¾ inches

Happy Holidays Needle Roll

Anchor		DMC	
212	⊠	561	Seafoam
045	♥	814	Garnet
	◯	002	Kreinik Gold #4 very-fine braid

BACKSTITCH (2X)

212	╱	561	Seafoam – "Happy Holidays"

SATIN STITCH (1X)

	·‖‖·	851	Needle Necessities Christmas Eve #8 pearl cotton

DIAMOND EYELET (2X)

045	✳	814	Garnet

SMYRNA CROSS-STITCH (1X)

212	✳	561	Seafoam
	✳	002	Kreinik Gold #4 very-fine braid

MILL HILL BEADS

	◦	02011	Victorian gold seed bead
	●	02012	Royal plum seed bead

Stitch count: 57 high x 60 wide

Finished design sizes:
28-count fabric – 4 x 4¼ inches
32-count fabric – 3½ x 3¾ inches
36-count fabric – 3⅛ x 3⅓ inches

Candle Banding

Caron Collection

♥	2071	Wildflowers Solid coral red thread
⊠	5011	Wildflowers Solid moss green thread
◯	002	Kreinik Gold #4 very-fine braid

SMYRNA CROSS-STITCH (1X)

✳	025	Wildflowers Holiday overdyed thread

DIAMOND EYELET (1X)

✳	2071	Wildflowers Solid coral red thread

MILL HILL BEADS

●	02013	Red red glass seed bead

Stitch count: 23 high x 120 wide

Finished design sizes:
28-count fabric – 1⅝ x 8½ inches
32-count fabric – 1½ x 7½ inches
36-count fabric – 1¼ x 6⅔ inches

Simply Samplers

Stitches

Center and stitch the design from the chart on the fabric. Use two plies of floss or one strand of braid to work the stitches over two threads of the fabric unless otherwise specified. When working with overdyed floss, complete each individual stitch before proceeding to the next one. Attach the seed beads using two plies of floss. Press the finished stitchery facedown on a soft towel.

Assembly

Centering the design, trim the stitchery ½" beyond the outermost stitches to make a square. Fuse the fleece to the back of the stitchery following the manufacturer's instructions.

Use the pillow front as a pattern to cut a matching back from the purple fabric. Also cut a 2½×45" piping strip from the purple fabric. Cut a 1¾×45" piping strip from the burgundy fabric.

Center the cording lengthwise on the wrong side of the piping strip. Fold the fabric over the cording, with the long edges together. Using a zipper foot, sew close to the cording through all layers. Sew the burgundy piping around the perimeter of the pillow front with raw edges even. Sew the purple piping around the pillow front behind the burgundy piping.

Sew the pillow front and back together with right sides facing and raw edges even, leaving an opening for turning. Trim the seams, clip the corners, and turn right side out. Press the pillow carefully. Stuff the pillow firmly with polyester fiberfill and slip-stitch the opening closed.

Winter Bulbs

DMC variegated		Weeks Dyeworks overdyed floss
90	✳	2223 Saffron
51	♡	2226 Carrot
115	♥	2264 Garnet
102	✕	2333 Peoria purple
113	▣	2339 Blue bonnet
Anchor		DMC cotton floss
235	▦	414 Steel
398	▬	415 Pearl gray
Anchor Marlitt		DMC
800	▪	35200 White rayon floss

BACKSTITCH

235	╱	414 Steel – top of bulbs, bulb hangers (1X)
113	╱	2339 Weeks Dyeworks Blue bonnet – yellow ornament (2X)
800	╱	35200 White rayon floss – snowflakes and corners (1X)
	╱	002 Kreinik Gold #8 fine braid – purple ornament (1X)

ALGERIAN EYELETS (1X)
(8 legs over 4 threads)

800	✳	35200 White rayon floss – border, snowflake at center right
113	✳	2339 Weeks Dyeworks Blue bonnet – yellow ornament (2X)
	✳	002 Kreinik Gold #8 fine braid – purple and garnet bulbs

DIAMOND EYELETS (1X)
(8 legs over 8 threads)

800	✳	35200 White rayon floss – center snowflakes and corner squares
	✳	002 Kreinik Gold #8 fine braid – border and orange bulb

(16 legs over 16 threads)

	✴	002 Kreinik Gold #8 fine braid – blue bulb

SQUARE EYELET (1X)
(16 legs over 4 threads)

	✴	002 Kreinik Gold #8 fine braid – corner squares

HERRINGBONE STITCH (1X), *page 110*

	╱╲	002 Kreinik Gold #8 fine braid – garnet bulb

MILL HILL BEADS

	○	00557 Gold seed beads

Pillow stitch count: 121 high x 121 wide
Pillow finished design sizes:
28-count fabric – 8¾ x 8¾ inches
32-count fabric – 7½ x 7½ inches
36-count fabric – 6¾ x 6¾ inches

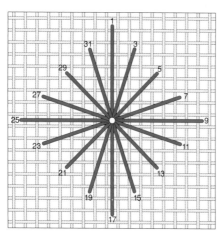

Diamond Eyelet

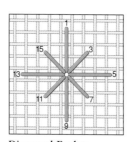

Diamond Eyelet

Algerian Eyelet

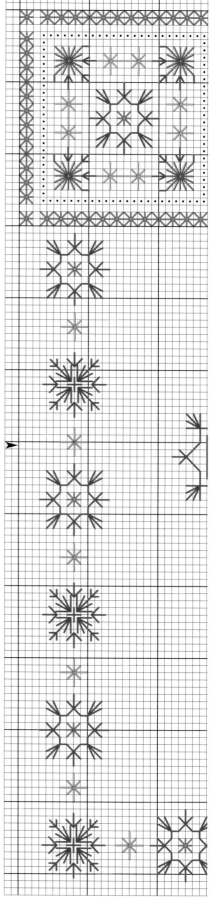

Winter Bulbs Pillow

Winter Bulbs Ornaments

Supplies

For each ornament
6" square of 14-count teal green
    Aida cloth
For each square ornament
Cotton embroidery floss
2½" square each of self-stick
    mounting board with foam and felt
12" length of purchased ¼"-diameter
    white piping
Kreinik 032 pearl #8 braid (hanger)
For the round ornaments
DMC variegated cotton floss
Kreinik #8 braid
3½" circle each of felt and self-stick
    mounting board with foam
9" length of purchased piping in
    desired color or 1×9" length of
    purple or burgundy cotton fabric and
    a 9" length of ⅛"-diameter cording

Stitches

Center and stitch the desired motif
from the chart, *pages 108–109,* on the
fabric. Use three plies of floss to work
the stitches unless otherwise
specified. When working with
variegated floss, work each stitch
separately before proceeding to the
next stitch. Place the stitchery
facedown on a soft towel and
carefully press from the back.

Assembly

Peel the protective paper from the
mounting board. Center the foam side
on the back of the stitchery and press
to stick. Trim the excess fabric
½" beyond the edge of the board.
Fold the edge of the fabric to the
back and glue in place.

Cover the cording in the same
manner as for the pillow. Position and
glue the piping around the edge of
the ornament, overlapping the ends at
the top center and trimming the
excess.

For the hanger, cut a 6" length of
#8 braid. Fold the braid in half to
form a loop. Glue the ends to the top
center of the ornament back. Glue the
felt to the back of the ornament.

Christmas in the Heart Bellpull

Supplies

14×16" piece of 28-count platinum
    Cashel linen
Cotton embroidery floss
Mill Hill seed beads
Mill Hill Treasures
4½×11" rectangle of tracing paper
6×12" piece of fusible fleece
6×12" piece of ivory cotton fabric
4½" brass bellpull hardware
24" length of ⅛"-diameter metallic
    gold cord
2—purchased 1½"-long metallic
    gold tassels
Purchased 3"-long metallic gold tassel

Stitches

Center and stitch the design on the
fabric. Use two plies of floss to work
the stitches over two threads of the
fabric unless otherwise specified. Refer
to the diagrams to work the remaining
stitches. Use one ply of floss to work
the lettering in half cross-stitches over
one thread of the fabric. Attach the
seed beads and the snowflake using
two plies of floss. Press the finished
stitchery facedown on a soft towel.

Assembly

To make the bellpull pattern, fold the
tracing paper in half lengthwise.
Measure 1½" from the bottom of the
paper and make a mark on the open
edge of the paper. At the center fold,
measure and mark a point ⅛" from the
bottom edge. With a ruler, connect the
marks with a diagonal line. Cut away
the excess paper at the drawn line.

Trace the pattern outline onto the
fleece; cut out. Position the fleece on
the back of the stitched piece with the
bottom point 1" below the bottom row
of stitches and centered side to side;
fuse. Cut away the excess linen ½"
beyond the fleece. Use the
stitchery as a pattern to cut a
matching back from the cotton fabric.

Sew the front and back together
with right sides together leaving the

top straight edge open for turning.
Trim the seams and clip the corners.
Turn right side out and press.

Press the raw edges to the inside
¼" and slip-stitch the opening closed.
Turn the top edge under 1" and hand-
stitch the edge to the back to make a
casing. Unscrew the finial from the
hardware. Slip the hardware through
the casing; replace the finial. Sew a
1½" tassel to each end of the cord
and tie the ends around the bellpull
hardware. Hand-sew the 3" tassel to
the bottom point of the bellpull.

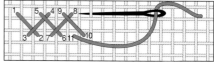

Long-Arm Cross-Stitch

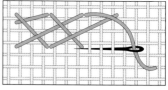

Rice Stitch over 6

Algerian Eyelet

Herringbone Stitch over 2

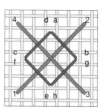

Star Stitch over 4

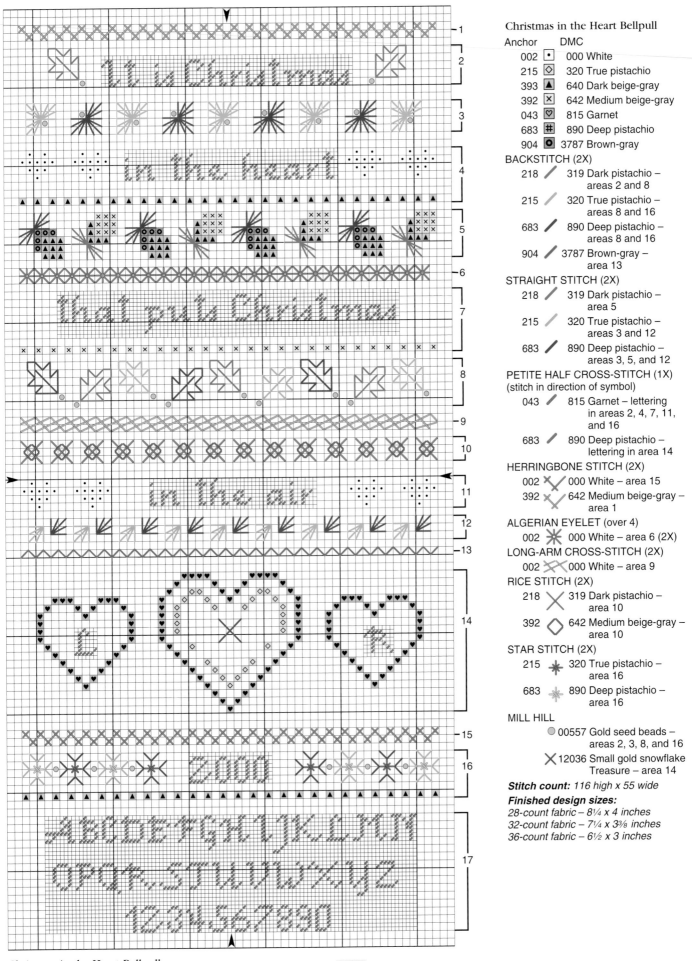

Christmas in the Heart Bellpull

Anchor	DMC	
002	•	000 White
215	◇	320 True pistachio
393	▲	640 Dark beige-gray
392	✕	642 Medium beige-gray
043	♡	815 Garnet
683	#	890 Deep pistachio
904	◉	3787 Brown-gray

BACKSTITCH (2X)

218	/	319 Dark pistachio – areas 2 and 8
215	/	320 True pistachio – areas 8 and 16
683	/	890 Deep pistachio – areas 8 and 16
904	/	3787 Brown-gray – area 13

STRAIGHT STITCH (2X)

218	/	319 Dark pistachio – area 5
215	/	320 True pistachio – areas 3 and 12
683	/	890 Deep pistachio – areas 3, 5, and 12

PETITE HALF CROSS-STITCH (1X)
(stitch in direction of symbol)

| 043 | / | 815 Garnet – lettering in areas 2, 4, 7, 11, and 16 |
| 683 | / | 890 Deep pistachio – lettering in area 14 |

HERRINGBONE STITCH (2X)

| 002 | ✕/ | 000 White – area 15 |
| 392 | ✕/ | 642 Medium beige-gray – area 1 |

ALGERIAN EYELET (over 4)

| 002 | ✳ | 000 White – area 6 (2X) |

LONG-ARM CROSS-STITCH (2X)

| 002 | ✕✕ | 000 White – area 9 |

RICE STITCH (2X)

| 218 | ✕ | 319 Dark pistachio – area 10 |
| 392 | ◇ | 642 Medium beige-gray – area 10 |

STAR STITCH (2X)

| 215 | ✳ | 320 True pistachio – area 16 |
| 683 | ✳ | 890 Deep pistachio – area 16 |

MILL HILL

| ● | 00557 Gold seed beads – areas 2, 3, 8, and 16 |
| ✕ | 12036 Small gold snowflake Treasure – area 14 |

Stitch count: *116 high x 55 wide*
Finished design sizes:
28-count fabric – 8¼ x 4 inches
32-count fabric – 7¼ x 3⅜ inches
36-count fabric – 6½ x 3 inches

Christmas in the Heart Bellpull

Simply Samplers

*N*o matter how busy
the holidays become,

you can find time

to create these

hand-stitched trims

and gifts.

~

Quick and Merry

*A*ll you really need for a merry Christmas is one good collection

of cross-stitch motifs. Stitch this easy piece on 14-count Aida cloth to frame and display throughout

the season. The small designs can be stitched on a variety of other fabrics, including perforated paper.

*S*titch A winter wonderland with white floss on green or red fabric.

The silhouette design allows you to be creative, and your fabric choice determines the size. Stitch a

medium stocking on 14-count Aida cloth or make it grandiose on 21-count Vienna fabric.

Designs: I Will Keep Christmas, Robin Kingsley; Winter Wonderland Stockings, Jim Williams

A simple snowflake, stitched in

your choice of shiny braid colors on metallic perforated paper,

is versatile. Add a shiny tassel for an tree ornament, attach one to some pretty ribbon to make

a napkin ring, or mount it on shiny card stock for a greeting card or package tie.

Glistening beads, lacy lines of backstitching, and a few cross-stitches

combine to make lovely ornaments worked on 14-count Aida cloth. For an elegant gift, enlarge

either design on 10-count linen and finish as a journal cover.

Designs: Gold Dust Snowflakes, Linda Clark; Beads and Lace, Ursula Michael

Quick and Merry

*E*ven when time is short, stitch up colorful

ornaments that depict traditional Christmas toys.

Finish each one in a simple shape and surround it with

purchased piping in a primary color.

Designs: Toy Ornaments, Studio B

I Will Keep Christmas

Supplies
14×16" piece of 11-count white
  Aida cloth
Cotton embroidery floss
Desired frame

Stitches
Center and stitch the design on the
fabric. Use four plies of floss to work
the stitches unless otherwise specified.
Press the stitchery from the back.
Frame the piece as desired.

Anchor		DMC	
002	·	000	White
1049	◆	301	Mahogany
011	✕	350	Medium coral
923	★	699	Dark Christmas green
227	+	701	True Christmas green
257	/	703	Chartreuse
305	△	725	Topaz
868	−	754	Peach
140	☆	813	Powder blue
047	♥	817	Deep coral
161	◯	826	Bright blue
382	■	3371	Black-brown

BACKSTITCH
923	/	699	Dark Christmas green – plaid heart (1X)
047	/	817	Deep coral – merry (2X)
382	/	3371	Black-brown – lettering (2X), all other stitches (1X)

FRENCH KNOT (2X wrapped once)
047	●	817	Deep coral – Santa's nose and mouth
382	●	3371	Black-brown – lettering, snowman eyes and buttons, Santa's eyes

I Will Keep Christmas

Stitch count: *84 high x 56 wide*
Finished design sizes:
11-count fabric – 7⅝ x 5 inches
14-count fabric – 6 x 4 inches
16-count fabric – 5¼ x 3½ inches
Snowman stitch count: *19 high x 16 wide*
Snowman finished design sizes:
14-count fabric – 1⅓ x 1⅛ inches

Stocking stitch count: *21 high x 20 wide*
Stocking finished design sizes:
14-count fabric – 1½ x 1½ inches
Santa stitch count: *33 high x 25 wide*
Santa finished design sizes:
14-count fabric – 2⅓ x 1¾ inches

I Will Keep Christmas Package Tags

Supplies

For each tag
3" square of 14-count white
    perforated paper
Cotton embroidery floss
Solid red, solid green, and
    white-and-red print vellum paper
6" length of fine braid
Crafts glue

Stitches

Center and stitch the desired motif from the chart, *page 119,* on the perforated paper. Use two plies of floss to work the cross-stitches. Work the backstitches using one ply of floss. Cut out the shape one square beyond the stitched area.

Assembly

Cut squares in graduated sizes from the vellum paper. Center and glue the stitched shape to the center of a red vellum square. Glue a second, slightly larger square in a contrasting color to the back of the red square. Turn the squares diagonally to vary the look of the finished ornament. See the photograph on *page 114* for additional ideas. For the hanger, thread the braid through the top of the ornament.

Winter Wonderland Stockings

The large stocking is 15" long. The small stocking is 11½" long.

Supplies

For the large stocking
21×18" piece of 21-count red
    Vienna fabric
Cotton embroidery floss
19×16" piece of fusible fleece
⅝ yard of 45"-wide red
    cotton fabric
1¼ yards of ¼"-diameter
    cording
For the medium stocking
18×14" piece of 14-count
    green Aida cloth
Cotton embroidery floss
16×11" piece of fusible fleece
1 yard of ⅛"- diameter
    cording
½ yard of 45"-wide green
    cotton fabric

Stitches

Center and stitch the design on the desired fabric. Use three plies of floss to work the cross-stitches over two threads of the Vienna fabric or one square of Aida cloth. Work the backstitches as specified. Press the finished stitchery from the back.

Assembly

For both stockings, fuse the fleece to the back of the stitched piece following the manufacturer's instructions. Use the erasable marker to draw the stocking outline as indicated by the dashed line on the chart. Cut out the stocking ½" beyond the marked line. Use the stocking as a pattern to cut a matching back and two lining pieces from the matching cotton fabric.

For the large stocking, cut a 1⅞×44" piping strip and a 1⅝×5" hanging strip from the red fabric.

For the small stocking, cut a 1½×36" piping strip and a 1¼"×4" hanging strip from the green fabric.

For both stockings, center the cording lengthwise on the wrong side of the piping strip. Fold the fabric around the cording with raw edges

together. Use a zipper foot to sew through both layers close to the cording. Baste the piping around the stocking's sides and foot with the raw edges even.

Press the long edges of the hanging strip under ¼", fold in half lengthwise, and topstitch. Fold the strip in half to form a loop. Tack the ends inside the top right side of the stocking.

With right sides together, using the zipper foot, sew the stocking front to the back with a ½" seam allowance, leaving the top edge open. Trim the seam allowance to ¼". For curves, clip the piping seam allowance frequently until the piping lies flat.

Turn the stocking right side out and press. Sew the lining pieces together, right sides together; *do not* turn. Slip the stocking inside the lining. Stitch the stocking and the lining together at the top edges with right sides together; turn right side out. Slip-stitch the opening closed. Tuck the lining into the stocking, and press carefully.

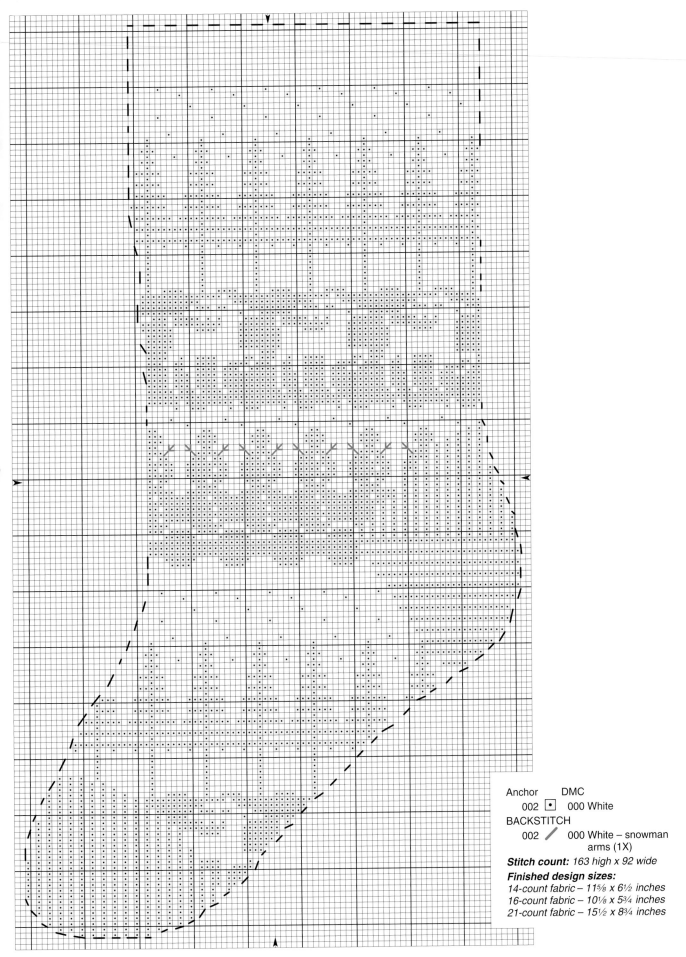

Anchor | | DMC
002 | ⊡ | 000 White

BACKSTITCH

002 | ╱ | 000 White – snowman
| | arms (1X)

Stitch count: *163 high x 92 wide*
Finished design sizes:
14-count fabric – 11⅝ x 6½ inches
16-count fabric – 10⅛ x 5¾ inches
21-count fabric – 15½ x 8¾ inches

Winter Wonderland Stockings

Gold Dust Snowflake Card and Ornament

Supplies
3" square of 14-count white, silver, or gold perforated paper
2½" square of 14-count silver or gold perforated paper
Kreinik #4 and #8 braid
Purchased 1½"-long metallic gold tassel or a 4¼×7½" piece of metallic cardstock
Crafts glue

Stitches
Center and stitch the design from the chart on the desired 3" square of perforated paper using the desired color key. Use one strand of braid to work the stitches. Centering the design, trim the finished stitchery to a 1¼" square.

Assembly
For the ornament, glue the tassel to one corner of the stitchery. Center and glue the stitched square atop a 2½" gold or silver square of perforated paper. For the hanger, thread a 12" length of braid through the top of the ornament; knot the braid ends.

For the cards, center and glue the stitched square atop a 2½" gold or silver square of perforated paper. Fold the cardstock in half to make a 3¾×4¼" rectangle. Position the stitchery atop the front of the card as desired, and glue in place.

Beads and Lace Journal

Supplies
8" square of 10-count white Betsy Ross linen
Rayon or cotton embroidery floss
Mill Hill seed beads and Treasures
10×18" piece of lightweight fusible interfacing
10×18" piece of blue nonwoven art paper
6" square of paper-backed fusible webbing
Purchased blank journal
Pinking shears
Spray adhesive
Crafts glue

Stitches
Center and stitch the design from the chart on the fabric. Use four plies of floss to work the stitches unless otherwise specified. Press the stitchery from the back.

Assembly
Make a pattern for the book cover by tracing around the open book on the interfacing; cut out 1" beyond the traced line.

Fuse the interfacing to the back of the art paper following the manufacturer's instructions. Fold the long edges of the cover under 1"; glue. Spray the outside of the journal lightly with the adhesive and position the cover on top. Fold the ends of the paper to the inside of the book and glue them in place.

Center and fuse the webbing to the back of the stitchery following the manufacturer's instructions. Use two plies of floss to attach the star at the position indicated on the chart. Centering the design, trim the fabric to a 5" square with pinking shears. Remove the paper backing from the fusible webbing. Center the stitched piece on the book front about 1½" from the top. Working around the star, fuse the stitched piece in place.

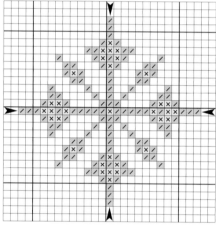

Gold Dust Snowflake Card and Ornament

Gold Dust Snowflake Card and Ornament
(Plum Version)

Kreinik Braid
- ☒ 002 Gold #4 very-fine braid
- ☑ 1223 Passion plum #8 fine braid

Gold Dust Snowflake Card and Ornament
(Red Version)

Kreinik Braid
- ☒ 002 Gold #4 very-fine braid
- ☑ 326 Hibiscus #8 fine braid

Gold Dust Snowflake Card and Ornament
(Blue Version)

Kreinik Braid
- ☒ 002 Gold #4 very-fine braid
- ☑ 393 Silver night #8 fine braid

Gold Dust Snowflake Card and Ornament
(Green Version)

Kreinik Braid
- ☒ 002 Gold #4 very-fine braid
- ☑ 070 Mardi Gras #8 fine braid

Stitch count: 25 high x 25 wide
Finished design sizes:
14-count fabric – 1¾ x 1¾ inches
16-count fabric – 1½ x 1½ inches
18-count fabric – 1⅓ x 1⅓ inches

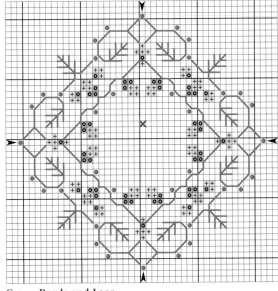

Anchor	DMC	Marlitt		DMC Rayon	
228	700	852	◉	30700	Christmas green
256	704	058	⊞	30704	Chartreuse
BACKSTITCH					
188	943	1055	╱	30943	Aqua
MILL HILL BEADS					
			✖	12175	Opal bright small flat star
			●	02013	Red red seed beads

Stitch count: 43 high x 43 wide
Finished design sizes:
14-count fabric – 3⅛ x 3⅛ inches
16-count fabric – 2⅝ x 2⅝ inches
18-count fabric – 2⅓ x 2⅓ inches

Green Beads and Lace

Anchor	DMC	Marlitt		DMC Rayon	
090	554	816	⊟	30554	Violet
136	799	1009	✖	30799	Delft blue
BACKSTITCH					
188	943	1055	╱	30943	Aqua
MILL HILL BEADS					
			✖	13059	Crystal AB star
			●	62020	Frosted Creme de mint seed beads

Stitch count: 41 high x 41 wide
Finished design sizes:
14-count fabric – 3 x 3 inches
16-count fabric – 2½ x 2½ inches
18-count fabric – 2¼ x 2¼ inches

Blue Beads and Lace

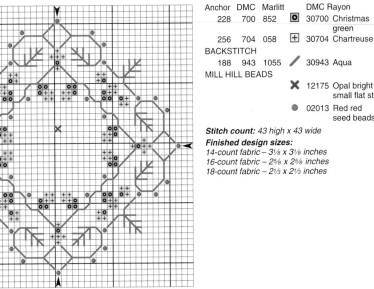

Beads and Lace Ornaments

Supplies

For each ornament
8″ square of 14-count white Aida cloth
Rayon or cotton embroidery floss
Mill Hill seed beads and Treasures
3⅝″ circle of self-stick mounting board
  with foam
3⅝″ circle of white felt
Crafts glue

Stitches

Center and stitch the design on the Aida cloth. Use two plies of floss to work the stitches unless otherwise specified. Attach the seed beads and Treasure using two plies of floss. Press the finished stitchery facedown on a soft towel.

Assembly

Peel the protective paper from the mounting board. Center the foam side on the back of the stitchery and press to stick. Trim the excess fabric ½″ beyond the edge of the board. Fold the edge of the fabric to the back and glue in place.

For the hanger, cut two 14″ lengths of aqua floss (DMC 30943). Combine the plies into a single 12-ply strand. Secure one end of the joined strands and twist until tightly wound. Holding the ends, fold the strand in half as the two halves twist around each other. Fold the twisted cord in half to form a loop. Glue the cord ends to the top center of the ornament back.

For the twisted cord edging, cut two 36″-long six-ply lengths of aqua floss (DMC 30943). Combine the plies and twist as directed above.

Position and glue the cord around the edge of the ornament, overlapping the ends at the top center and trimming the excess. Glue the felt to the back of the ornament.

Quick and Merry

Toy Ornaments

Anchor		DMC	
002	•	000	White
110	♦	208	Dark lavender
109	✕	209	Medium lavender
1006	♡	304	Christmas red
403	■	310	Black
063	☆	602	Medium cranberry
075	−	604	Light cranberry
046	#	666	Red
316	◉	740	Dark tangerine
304	☐	741	Medium tangerine
303	+	742	Light tangerine
301	‖	744	Yellow
868	╱	754	Peach
229	▲	909	Dark emerald
228	◇	910	True emerald
204	○	913	Nile green
1034	⊟	931	Antique blue
355	◉	975	Deep golden brown
1001	▽	976	Medium golden brown
410	★	995	Dark electric blue
433	⌃	996	Light electric blue

BACKSTITCH

110	╱	208	Dark lavender – doll's hair bows (2X)
1006	╱	304	Christmas red – doll's mouth (1X)
403	╱	310	Black – lettering on train, trim on soldier's jacket (1X)
228	╱	910	Dark emerald – flower stems on doll's dress (1X)
355	╱	975	Deep golden brown – reindeer (1X)
382	╱	3371	Black-brown – all other stitches (1X)

LAZY DAISY

110	⬮	208	Dark lavender – doll's hair bows (2X)

FRENCH KNOT

403	●	310	Black – doll and soldier's eyes, trim on soldier's jacket (1X wrapped once); jack-in-box eyes (1X wrapped twice)

BUTTON PLACEMENT

⊕ ⅛"-diameter button – soldier's hat, doll clothing

⊕ ¼"-diameter button – soldier's jacket

⊕ ⅜"-diameter button – jack-in-box, train wheel

Toy Ornaments

Supplies

For each ornament
10" square of 14-count white Aida cloth
Cotton embroidery floss
Assorted buttons
Tracing paper; erasable fabric marker
6" square each of self-stick mounting board with foam and white felt
15" length of ⅛"-diameter piping
6" length of ⅛"-wide satin ribbon
Crafts glue

Stitches

Center and stitch the design on the Aida cloth. Use three plies of floss to work the stitches unless otherwise specified. Use matching floss to attach the buttons. Press from the back.

Assembly

Use the erasable marker to draw an outline around the stitched area of the

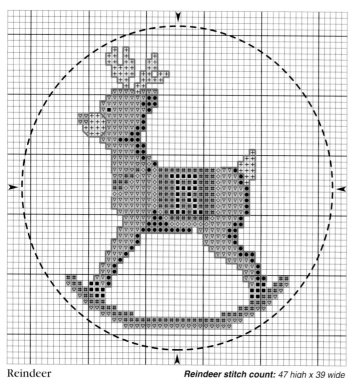

Reindeer

Reindeer stitch count: 47 high x 39 wide
Reindeer finished design sizes:
14-count fabric – 3⅓ x 2¾ inches
16-count fabric – 3 x 2½ inches
18-count fabric – 2⅔ x 2⅛ inches

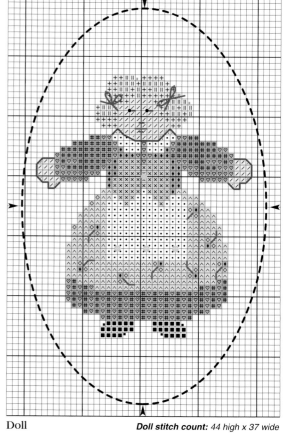

Doll

Doll stitch count: 44 high x 37 wide
Doll finished design sizes:
14-count fabric – 3⅛ x 2⅝ inches
16-count fabric – 2¾ x 2⅓ inches
18-count fabric – 2½ x 2 inches

design as indicated by the dashed line on the chart; *do not* cut out. Place the tracing paper over the fabric and trace the ornament outline. Cut out the paper pattern. Use the paper pattern to cut matching shapes from the mounting board and the felt.

Peel the protective paper from the mounting board. Center the foam side on the back of the stitchery and press to stick. Trim the excess fabric ½" beyond the edge of the board. Fold the edge of the fabric to the back and glue in place.

Position and glue the piping around the edge of the ornament, overlapping the ends at the top center and trimming the excess.

For the hanger, fold the 6" length of ribbon in half to form a loop. Glue the ribbon ends to the top center of the ornament back. Glue the felt to the back of the ornament.

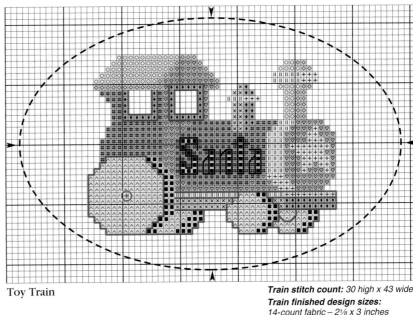

Toy Train

Train stitch count: 30 high x 43 wide
Train finished design sizes:
14-count fabric – 2⅛ x 3 inches
16-count fabric – 1⅞ x 2⅔ inches
18-count fabric – 1⅔ x 2⅜ inches

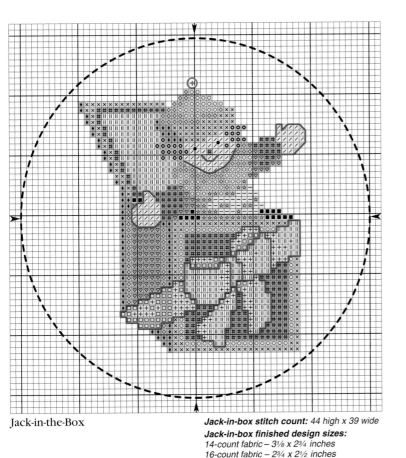

Jack-in-the-Box

Jack-in-box stitch count: 44 high x 39 wide
Jack-in-box finished design sizes:
14-count fabric – 3⅛ x 2¾ inches
16-count fabric – 2¾ x 2½ inches
18-count fabric – 2½ x 2⅛ inches

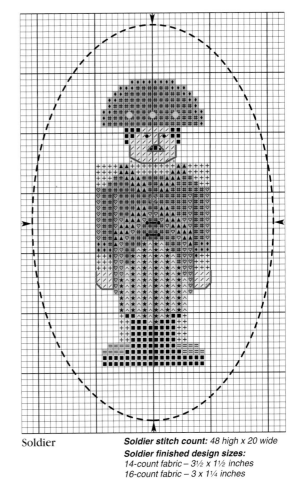

Soldier

Soldier stitch count: 48 high x 20 wide
Soldier finished design sizes:
14-count fabric – 3½ x 1½ inches
16-count fabric – 3 x 1¼ inches
18-count fabric – 2⅔ x 1⅛ inches

Quick and Merry

Cross-Stitch Basics

Getting started

For most projects in this book, the starting point is at the center of both the chart and the fabric. Every chart has arrows that indicate the horizontal and vertical centers. With your finger, trace along the grid to the point where the two centers meet. Compare a symbol at the center of the chart to the key and choose which floss color to stitch first. To find the center of the fabric, fold it into quarters and finger-crease or baste along the folds with a single ply of contrasting floss.

Cut the floss into 15" to 18" lengths, and separate all six plies. Recombine the plies as indicated in the project instructions, and thread them into a blunt-tip needle.

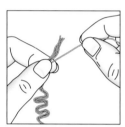

Separating Floss

Basic cross-stitch

Make one cross-stitch for each symbol on the chart. For horizontal rows, stitch the first diagonal of each stitch in the row. Then work back across the row, completing each stitch. On most linen and even-weave fabrics, work your stitches over two threads as shown in the diagram below. For Aida cloth, each stitch fills one square.

You also can work cross-stitches in the reverse direction. Just remember to embroider the stitches uniformly—that is, always work the top half of each stitch in the same direction.

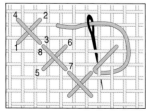

Cross-Stitch Worked Singly

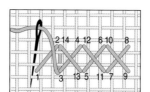

Cross-Stitch Worked in Rows

To secure thread at the beginning

The most common way to secure the beginning tail of the thread is to hold it in place on the back side while working the first four or five stitches over it.

To secure the thread with a waste knot, thread the needle and knot the end of the thread. Insert the needle from the right side of the fabric, about 4 inches away from the first stitch. Bring the needle up through the fabric, and work the first series of stitches. When finished, clip the knot on the right side. Rethread the needle with excess floss and push the needle through to the stitches on the wrong side of the fabric.

When you work with two, four, or six plies of floss, use a loop knot. Cut half as many plies of thread, but make each one twice as long. Recombine the plies, fold the strand in half, and thread all of the ends into the needle. Work the first diagonal of the first stitch, then slip the needle through the loop formed by folding the thread.

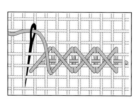

To Secure Thread at the Beginning

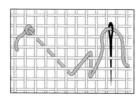

To Secure Thread with a Waste Knot

To secure thread at the end

To finish, slip the threaded needle under previously stitched threads on the wrong side of the fabric for four or five stitches, weaving the thread back and forth a few times. Clip the thread.

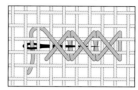

To Secure Thread at the End

Quarter and three-quarter cross-stitches

To obtain rounded shapes in a design, use quarter and three-quarter cross-stitches. On linen and evenweave fabrics, a quarter cross-stitch will extend from the corner to the center intersection of the threads. To make quarter cross-stitches on Aida cloth, estimate the center of the square. Three-quarter cross-stitches combine a quarter cross-stitch with a half cross-stitch. Both stitches may slant in any direction.

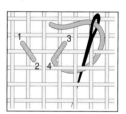

Quarter Cross-Stitch

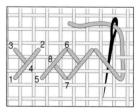

Three-Quarter Cross-Stitch

Backstitches

Backstitches define and outline the shapes in a design. For most projects, backstitches require only one ply of floss. On the color key, (2X) indicates two plies of floss, (3X) indicates three plies, etc. ◁

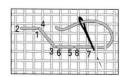

Backstitch

Index

Sources

Many of the materials and items used in this book are available at crafts and needlework stores. For more information, write or call the manufacturers listed below.

CHRISTMAS PAST AND PRESENT

Hardanger Bellpull, *page 8:* Jobelan fabric—Wichelt Imports, Inc. Seed beads—Mill Hill. Bellpull hardware—Norden Crafts, Ltd., www.nordencrafts.com.

Postcard Santa, *page 9:* Olive green Cashel linen—Zweigart.

Blackwork Ornaments, *page 10:* Jobelan fabric—Wichelt Imports, Inc.

Canaries and Pinecones, *pages 10–11:* Lugana fabric—Zweigart. Edinburgh linen—Wichelt Imports, Inc., Zweigart. Satin ribbon—C.M. Offray & Sons, Inc., Route 24, Box 601, Chester, NJ 07930; 908/879-4700.

Blue and Green Santas, *pages 12–13:* Natural light linen—Wichelt Imports, Inc.

Victorian Monograms, *pages 14–15:* Bonnie blue, cherub pink, and English mist linen—Wichelt Imports, Inc. Friendship blue linen—R&R Reproductions. Aida banding—Mill Hill. Purse hardware—Lacis, 3163 Adeline St., Berkeley, CA 94703; www.lacis.com. Overdyed floss—Needle Necessities, Inc. Rubber stamp—Hot Potatoes, 2805 Columbine Pl., Nashville, TN 37204; www.hotpotatoes.com, 615/269-8002.

HIGH-SPIRITED HOLIDAYS

Christmas Alphabet, *pages 34–35:* Aida cloth—Charles Craft, Wichelt Imports, Inc., Zweigart.

Believe in the Magic, *page 36–37:* Aida cloth—Charles Craft, Wichelt Imports, Inc., Zweigart. Valerie fabric—Zweigart.

I Love Santa, *pages 38–39:* Heatherfield fabric—Wichelt Imports, Inc., Tula fabric—Zweigart.

Baby Stocking, *page 40:* Wool Aida cloth—Zweigart.

Hatching Christmas Cheer, *page 41:* Aida cloth—Charles Craft, Wichelt Imports, Inc., Zweigart.

Hoe! Hoe! Hoe! Stocking, *pages 42–43:* Royal Classic fabric—Charles Craft. Aida banding—Zweigart.

CHRISTMAS IS LOVE

Love Came Down at Christmas Sampler, *page 64:* Belfast linen—Zweigart.

Faith Angel, *page 65:* Jobelan fabric—Wichelt Imports, Inc.

Heart of Christmas Pillows, *page 66:* Aida cloth—Charles Craft, Wichelt Imports, Inc., Zweigart. Aida banding—Zweigart.

Nativity, *page 67:* Jobelan fabric—Wichelt Imports, Inc.

Mistlesnow People, *page 68:* Aida cloth—Zweigart.

Heart Wreath and Ornament, *page 69:* Aida cloth—Charles Craft, Wichelt Imports, Inc., Zweigart. Perforated paper—Yarn Tree Designs. Ribbon—Mokuba, MKB Ribbon, 212/302-5010; www.exquisite-ribbon.com or JKM Products, 856/757-6604.

FESTIVE FOLK ART

Folk Art Ornaments, *page 85:* Sandstone linen—Wichelt Imports, Inc.

O' Christmas Tree Pillow, *page 85:* Natural linen—Wichelt Imports, Inc.

Sampler Hearts Ornaments, *page 86:* Fiddler's Lite Aida cloth—Charles Craft.

Merry Little Christmas, *page 87:* Navy Aida cloth—Wichelt Imports, Inc., Zweigart. Overdyed floss—The Gentle Art.

I'll Be Home for Christmas, *page 88:* Rosemary linen—Wichelt Imports, Inc.

SIMPLY SAMPLERS

Poinsettia Sampler, *page 98:* Laurel linen—Wichelt Imports, Inc.

Christmas Joy Sampler, *page 99:* Lambswool linen—Wichelt Imports, Inc. Overdyed floss—The Gentle Art. Charm—Shepherd's Bush, 220 24th St., Ogden, UT 84401.

Holiday Greetings, *pages 100–101:* Star sapphire linen—Wichelt Imports, Inc.; Linen banding—Mill Hill. Ivory linen—Wichelt Imports, Inc. Overdyed pearl cotton—Needle Necessities; Waterlilies overdyed silk floss and Wildflowers thread—The Caron Collection.

Winter Balls Pillow and Ornaments, *pages 102–103:* Dark teal Cashel linen—Zweigart. Overdyed floss—Weeks Dyeworks. Teal green Aida cloth—Zweigart.

Christmas in the Heart Bellpull, *page 104:* Platinum Cashel linen—Zweigart. Bellpull hardware—Yarn Tree Designs.

EXTRA EASY

I Will Keep Christmas in My Heart, *page 114:* Aida cloth—Charles Craft, Wichelt Imports, Inc., Zweigart. Perforated paper—Yarn Tree Designs.

Winter Wonderland Stockings, *page 115:* Red Vienna fabric—Zweigart. Green Aida cloth—Wichelt Imports, Inc.

Gold Dust Cards and Ornament, *page 116:* Perforated paper—Yarn Tree Designs. Ribbon—Mokuba.

Beads and Lace, *page 117:* Aida cloth—Charles Craft, Wichelt Imports, Inc., Zweigart. Ribbon—Midori, Inc., www.midoriribbon.com, 800/659-3049.

Toy Ornaments, *page 118:* Aida cloth—Charles Craft, Wichelt Imports, Inc., Zweigart.

FABRICS

Charles Craft, P.O. Box 1049, Laurinburg, NC 28253; www.charlescraft.com.

R&R Reproductions, In Stitches, 8800–F Pear Tree Ct., Alexandria, VA 22309; 877/360-4600.

Wichelt Imports, Inc., Rte. 1, Stoddard, WI 54658; www.wichelt.com.

Yarn Tree Designs, 117 Alexander St., P.O. Box 724, Ames, IA 50010; www.yarntree.com, 800/247-3952.

Zweigart, 2 Riverview Dr., Somerset, NJ 08873-1139; www.zweigart.com, 732/271-1949.

THREADS

Anchor, Consumer Service Dept., P.O. Box 12229, Greenville, SC 29612; www.coatsandclark.com.

The Caron Collection, 55 Old South Ave., Stratford, CT 06615; www.caron-net.com, 203/381-9999.

DMC, Port Kearney Bldg. 10, South Kearney, NJ 07032-0650; www.dmc-usa.com.

The Gentle Art, 4081 Bremo Recess, New Albany, OH 43054, e-mail: gentleart@aol.com, 614/855-8346, fax 614/855-4298.

Kreinik Manufacturing Co., Inc., 800/537-2166 or Daisy Chain, P.O. Box 1258, Parkersburg, WV 26102, www.kreinik.com, 304/428-9500.

Needle Necessities, Inc., 7211 Garden Grove Blvd. #BC, Garden Grove, CA 92841; 800/542-7300.

Weeks Dyeworks, 404 Raleigh St., Fuquay-Varina, NC 27526-2233; www.weeksdyeworks.com.

BEADS

Mill Hill, www.millhillbeads.com, 800/447-1332.

Sabina baccata altera.

Arbor Vitæ siue Cedrus Lycia.

Iuniperus.

Cedrus phænicea